# Poems Of Emanshemet

The author is the middle child of three sisters and one brother. His Australian father left when Brian was ten years old and he lived in the family home for twenty-five years, living through very exciting War years.

The author's first job was in an engineering firm in London – a machine shop doing turning then as a draughtsman. Brian's first marriage was in the 60s and during this time he had extra work at Shepperton Studios. He was also employed as 'Special Skills' working with Bob Monkhouse, Shirley Eaton, Leslie Phillips and other 'Carry On' stars. The author gradually built up a business in vintage car dealing and made vintage specials for hill climbing car events. He then went on to buying and restoring period properties in London (when there were plenty about for under £10,000!). Brian's second relationship resulted in having three daughters but he eventually became a single parent throughout the 80s.

The author has experienced extreme hardships throughout his life. He moved to Forest Hill in the 90s then started writing seriously, having some poems published. Brian then moved to Littlehampton at the end of the 90s into a ramshackle Georgian house. His present occupation, besides writing, is building follies and garages from flint and old bricks. He also enjoys walking on the downs, church creeping, vintage cars (driving and restoring) and is part of a fraternity.

# Poems Of Emanshemet

Brian McDonell

# Poems Of Emanshemet

Olympia Publishers
*London*

www.olympiapublishers.com
OLYMPIA PAPERBACK EDITION

A CIP catalogue record for this title is
available from the British Library.

ISBN: 978-1-84897-242-1

This is a work of fiction.
Names, characters, places and incidents originate from the writer's
imagination. Any resemblance to actual persons, living or dead, is
purely coincidental.

**First Published in 2012**

Olympia Publishers
60 Cannon Street
London
EC4N 6NP


Printed in Great Britain

# Dedication

*To Steve Armstrong and the girls in my life*

# INDEX TO POEMS

# POEMS OF EMANSHEMET!

Emanshemet, Emanshemet
What the hell is that?
Not for Dons or Egg-heads
Or for Academics too
If you like a poetic fantasy
Then I've written it for you.
You possibly may rage
But it will make you think
Bound to make you laugh
And sure to make you cry
So do read Emanshemet
Some time before you die.


By Brian McDonell

# PRELUDE

Shall I drink to the girl that never I found?
She's just like the one next door
She's happy all day, I've watched her play
With her two little babies and more, and more
With her two little babies and more.

Is there a girl out there who's looking for me?
Did she raise an eye as I passed her by?
Did she then go home and lay on her bed
And say "What a wonderful guy, a guy
Oh, what a wonderful guy."

Is there a girl that could be mine?
Perhaps her partner's a bore
A simple sort of girl, one off the peg
Like the check-out girl at the store, the store
Like the check-out girl at the store.

Should I try for the darling that's spoken for?
She's a girl that I could steal
I'm a small fish in her pond, she wouldn't respond
And how could she know how I feel, I feel
How could she know how I feel?

So I'll drink to the girl that never I found
While dreaming of ways I could fill her with joy
I quite often see her out in the street
But she's always with some other boy, a boy
She's always with some other boy.

# 01

## <u>Happy Springtime</u>

Spring is here and dawn is breaking
The dreaming suburb slowly waking
Early cars come lurching, breaking
Over humps of council making.
Drakefield Gardens still is sleeping
By rows of cherry blossom peeping
Worms are caught in furious nesting
Dragged from earth with great protesting.
Birds do call from bush and flowers
To their mates in swaying towers
Squawking chicks in nests do fight
To relieve their endless appetite.
Soon the bees will swarm the flowers
Cashing in the sunny hour
Then the rush hour traffic roaring
To drown the sweet dawn chorus soaring.
Now the sun breaks free from night
Pouring out its golden light
Gilds the chimney pots on high
Lights the bedrooms and the sky.
Early risers from sleep are torn
Yet another day is born
London pigeons coo and pair
In the swiftly warming air.

Here's our Hero he is laying
In a house that's like a shed
He's asleep and safely dreaming
In his ancient wooden bed.

In a prefab, built by Yanks in forty-four
Where the bombs fell in the war
Oddly placed and by itself
Sure it's left there on the shelf
Strange that it should still stand
With the rising cost of land
But it does with privet hedges, tall and green
All around to make a screen.
Now he lives here with no other
Dead his father and his mother
Happy was he man and boy
For he was their love and joy.
There was a garden full of flowers
Where his father worked for hours
Now little of that glory's showing
But thistles ever quickly growing.
Buddleia takes the summer store
Fights it out with sycamore
Oh that lawn's a sad affair
Weeds and clover mostly there
Roses here and there do thrive
But forlorn and half alive
Just a moment here's our Hero, here he comes
From the front door spritely runs.
At seven thirty every day
Washed and shaved he makes his way
Full of longing and of joy
Light footed as a little boy
Now his heart is in a whirl
For soon he'll see his favourite girl.

# 02

## <u>Wishful Dreaming</u>

"I dream every night of her wonderful face
Then happiness follows me there
For I am hers, and she is mine
But only to wake in despair.
I'm soon back to sleep, there without pain
My head is drifting and dreaming again
I'm holding her hand, we kiss for awhile
In a faraway place, by a quaint country stile.
But mostly of closeness and her magical touch
Oh yes! I dream of that ever so much
There's giggles and banter as we walk for miles
She's all the time giving me promising smiles.
Alas! In the morning all is the same
I have been dreaming this all in vain
So today is the day I'll state my case
Or this is the end of a beautiful chase."

In his stomach butterflies are churning
In his head a song is stirring.

## 03

## <u>Could Two Stars Collide</u>

"I suppose I love her
Because she's so far out of reach
And there's not a chance in hell
I'll be needed at the breech.
Far more likely that in heaven
Two stars should collide
That this approaching figure
Could ever be my bride.
It's clear for anyone to see
God, she's much too good for me!
It's a comedy I chase her
And break my silly heart in two
It's a mystery why I do it
But I do!
I'm caught up in her sunlight
I think it's always shone
I don't know where I'm going
But I've gone!
Time is ripe to toss the dice
It may be a lot of fun
But I won't know what I'm doing
'til it's done!"

He's standing by the bus stop smiling
She's appearing much beguiling
Wow our Hero's aiming high
This girl's way up in the sky
Sweet and comely five foot high
With friendly devils in her eye

Flashing white bright open wide
And a bust line at high tide.
Her little dress leaves no surprises
For her legs could win first prizes
She moves about as if on wheels
And she were born with those high heels.
She overflows with joyful fun
That smile of hers outshines the sun
Why this girl's a little bunch of flowers
She could waste my time for hours.
Now our Hero's eyes are roving, tracing
And his heart is pounding, racing
His brain has just received a shunt
Feels upside down and back to front.
Try oh try as he might
All his words just don't come right
"Oh that's a nice mess you're tearing
Yes, nice the dress you're daring."
"Thanks," she says and beams politely
Nods her head and curtsies slightly
Such words to her are sweet as honey
They make her feel all good and funny.
Though she's dressed a little wild
Just inside there lurks a child
Clean and good and well presented
But her heart is easily dented.

Now they're on the bus that's churning
Fearful closeness swells his yearning
His poor heart is still full beat
And the words still incomplete.
Sits beside her broadly grinning
Hears her words that sound like singing
But this girl she talks non-stop

So scarcely can he get a shot
But at last he finds his words
For our Hero must be heard.

"What in all this world do you want most dearly?
Come tell me what it is sincerely."

# 04

## Asking Too Much Already

"Oh that is easy and won't ever change
But I'm afraid it covers quite a range
I want a man who's much like you
With a generous heart that is true.
No betting shops or smoky pubs
Fruit machines or money eating clubs
Not too proud to cook for me
Or too weak to put me over his knee.
A man that does just what he should
Who works in metal and in wood
He must love the trees and flowers
And know the ways of winds and showers.
To be at one with stars that shine
He's the man that I'll make mine
Strong in arm and clear in head
He'll be the one to share my bed!
Oh yes, there's something more
A little bit of cash in store
A little house that's strong and sure
With bright red roses over the door.
Then much happiness is all I'll sing
To my real golden wedding ring
Then we'd build a life uniquely ours
In fact I want a life of flowers."

Although our Hero's deeply shocked
His love for her is firmly locked
"Crikey!" He says with a stifle
"It looks as if I'll have no rival."

The bus has got to Peckham Rye
So this is where they say goodbye
He's in no particular rush
But she has to catch another bus
He runs along beside his treasure
Asking questions out of measure.

# 05

## Lucky Shot

"Would you go out with me dancing?"
She just gives him sidelong glancing
"Would you come to see a show?"
"Oh, I really don't know."
"Would you walk with me on the Rye tonight?"
"Not when the stars are shining bright."
"Come to Dulwich swimming there?"
"Not likely, that will spoil me hair."
"Do you like Indian? I could buy you some."
"Yes, but I'll have to ask me mum."
"Then would you come a-walking
"I could hold your hand?
"On Sunday we could go out walking
"Up in Dulwich wood."
"Oh I think I'd really like that
"But I don't know if I should."
"Please don't put yourself in a flurry
"Just say yes and don't you worry."
"Alright, yes, but take my warning
"I'll call on you, eleven Sunday morning."
Now he waves farewell with kisses
Some on target, some are misses
Then he turns for home again
But he's full of worries and in pain.

# 06

## **Second Thoughts**

"Countless times I've made this journey
Endless times I've risen early
To be so close to my desire
But hell it's now, I'm in a mire.
I'm just a plain and simple boy
What hope have I to find such joy?
What right have I to even try?
To get this angel in the sky.
I'm not a forward kind of fellow
In fact, I've even been called yellow
My nose is not the best of shape
My profile's very like an ape.
I'm not too smart or too tall
And at this moment feeling small
Maybe it's been a big mistake
And I'm nothing but a little fake
The years I feel do take their toll
But even worse I'm on the dole!"

As our Hero's homeward walking
Hears his mother's voice there talking
Feels the hand that rocked his cradle
With her wisdom and her fable.
"A feeble hearted man
Will never hold a beauty's hand
Few people if any
Ever get hold of the golden penny
If a rose her heart will woo
What more will a dozen do?"

Though the morning bright and warm
His head is in a kind of storm
Tired arms and legs like lead
He lies in silence on his bed.
With his problems he can't stay
His mind just wants to run away
There he wonders if he's able
To change his luck and turn the table
Into slumber he is falling
In his dream his mother calling
"A rose is no good without a smile
A smile will take you more than a mile."
Roses, roses that's the thing!!
Out the door and past the bin
Down the garden fresh from bed
Sorting out the garden shed
There's a fork and here's a shovel
Everything is in a muddle
Now our Hero's really working
There's no job that he is shirking.
Clears the garden with fork and hoe
With a huge and optimistic gusto
Trims the hedge, mows the lawn
Sweeps the path and burns the thorn.
By afternoon the job is done
And what he seeks he's found and won
Carefully lifted from the soil
This the triumph of his toil.
A climbing rose, quite ten feet high
With branches blotting out the sky
With all his strength and maybe more
He plants it by the entrance door.
Hell the thorns do tear him sadly

His sore hands are bleeding badly
But he ties the bush up neat and sure
Snugly frames his old front door.
With bowls of water on its roots
To ensure its buds and shoots
The sun is down, he washed and cleared away
This is the end of a long, long day.

Saturday morning he's looking busy
He rushes in a sort of tizzy
Cleans the windows shining bright
Paints the loo out gleaming white.
Off out shopping to Rye lane
Even though it starts to rain
Within an hour here he's coming
Up the hill he's almost running.
Armed with bags quite overflowing
With red roses plainly showing
It's a plan quite plain to see
And some kippers for his tea.
Oh those roses, bright red roses
All tied up in little posies
Each posy carefully wired tight
With a bag of water, out of sight
All afternoon with sores and pain
He works there in the pouring rain
Now the sullen clouds are going
And an evening sun is showing.
Indoors our Hero's feeling good
He's done all the things he could
Now he's eating kippers and bread
From the fish shop in Nunhead.
We leave our Hero inside dining
And the roses outside shining

I've always thought him rather lazy
This afternoon I thought him crazy.
I would apologise if I could
For that rose bower does look good
A shower of red roses, though I've got to say
There are a few other colours on display
But as for our Hero being bold
I think he really could win gold.

Blessed silent Sunday morning
All's asleep, but he's up yawning
Was the date she made for seven?
Or maybe it was set for eleven?
The sun is warm, the sky bright blue
So wait is all that he can do
At eight some distant bells are tolling
At nine the Sunday traffic's rolling.
At ten he can't wait anymore
And off he's rushing out the door
A thought that hit him like a bite
"Where was she on Saturday night?"
So to Selsey's own front door!
To sort it out and then be sure
Knocking loudly at the door
Comes a lady some four feet four.
She walks and speaks in little flurries
And seems consumed with dreadful worries
"Oh where is Selsey I need her badly?
Please understand I love her madly
You see she means the world to me
Just tell me all and set me free."
"Gaw, you're a weird one that's for sure
She's just left to see Emanshemet and nothing more."
"This Emanshemet Emanshemet

Where in hells name is that?!
Is it an opera or a ballet
Or a soap that's shown on telly."
"Gaw you're a bleedin' empty 'ead
A man she met I said!"
"Healing crystals! Up a tree
I thought she had a date with me."
"'ere," she says and grabs his arm
"Don't you do my Sel no 'arm."
But now he's running he has fled
To his house that's like a shed
Through the streets of Sunday yawning
Unseeing of the sunny morning.
He lies beneath his rosy bower
As church bells chime eleventh hour
Minutes come and slowly go
Each one like a hammer blow.
Drowsy sun is up and rising
From the roses, scent it's prizing
His head is throbbing by steaming sod
And soon he's in the land of nod.

**07**

## Under The Love Bower

Sprawled beneath his flowers dreaming
In a world of hope and seeming
In his dreaming eye he sees
Angels and the tops of trees.
Ever upward he is trying
To the light with angels flying
Swimming in a summer hue
Weightless in warm eternal blue.
But the angels spread their wings
Cast a shadow on his dreams
All with one accord they shout
"How dare you fly with us you lout!"
"Oh God in heaven I am falling
The wings I thought I had are stalling."
Swiftly downwards he is dropping
Then wakes to find his eyes are popping
But life down here is not so grim
An angel's kneeling over him.
He sees a flaming arc of red
The sun it hides behind her head
She is pleading, "Please don't die
Wake up now or I shall cry.
It's me, I'm here it's past eleven
Your roses here are just like heaven
The scent of roses makes me high
I'll always love them 'til I die.
You put this bush here in its place
There's more to you than a pretty face
Jump up please I'm full of yearning

For all of London's fields are burning.
Open places set me free
Like a sailor called by the sea."

Now they're off and gladly talking
Through the London streets are walking
Hand in hand and quite in love
As if they're guided from above.
Past the lofty walls of Nunhead
Up the darkened ivy passage
Walls are leaning all askew
Every verdant leaf brand new.
Now she gives a little shiver
For the chill flows like a river
At the top the sun's beguiling
Sunday afternoon is smiling.
Past the allotments things are growing
Old men busy weeding, hoeing
There the earth smells sweet and fresh
With rows of seedlings in their crèche.
Down the hill to Peckham Rye
Open space and big blue sky
They just pass, they're not staying
Noisy games of football playing.
Through the park all kissed with bloom
Rushing on they pass too soon
On to Brenchley Gardens alight with cherry flower
Far brighter than our Hero's bower.
Onto wooded One Tree Hill
Where once Queen Elizabeth filled the bill
So forever Honor Oak.

Now Selsey puffed and she's aglow
Although her limbs are white as snow
From the rucksack on her back
She produces wine and snack.
Eagerly they drink and eat
Staving off their thirst and heat
Now they're lying in the shadow
Of the church there of great height
Deep in long grass out of sight.
There they lay just the two
But he's unsure of what to do
Loving eyes they flash and shine
She has drunk most of the wine!
First his hand just strays a touch
Although he really wants to clutch
His heart is pounding, head is spinning
But now he really feels he's winning.
Suddenly there's nothing missing
They're so close they're almost kissing
Yes, life's as easy as a song
But in a flash it all goes wrong.
Quick get up the vicar's coming
Passing by them hymns he's humming
Now he's broken up their spell
Down the hill they run like hell.
Past the folly called Carron's Castle
With its views of Kent and Surrey
They run on, they're in a hurry
To the park at Hornimans, they're not staying
Until they hear the brass band playing.
They sit there in a little chair
By the bandstand in the sun
Just holding hands with her is fun
Bathed in light and drowned in sound

Their mutual peace is quite profound.

Songs from Westside Story
Now they're playing Land of Hope and Glory
As they're leaving Home Sweet Home
Drifts through the park like velvet foam.
Across the main road traffic pouring
With a thousand engines roaring
Through the gates of Cox's Walk
Now it's quiet they can talk.
Soon they're up in Dulwich Wood
A green and silent priceless wood
In her mind strange things are purring
Now her stomach oddly churning.

# 08

## The Grassy Ring

"Hero, hold me closer please
I must surrender to these trees
The scent, the breeze that whispers through the leaves
And faint hum of the bees.
All this far from the dreaded smoky din
Not to love here would be a sin
My head is foggy not from wine
This strange magic trickles down my spine.
Come deeper, deeper in the wood
Let's do the things that lovers should."
From the footpath they are running
Leaves and twigs are stinging, stunning
Then at some uncharted place
A little open sunlit space.
With smiling lips and sparkling eyes
She throws her rucksack to the skies
Then she begins to prance and spin
Encircling the grassy ring.
Her version of the seven veils
Poor Hero's head is off its rails
Flushed and glowing and she's not slowing
Ever faster she is going.
She is even more entrancing
Clothes are shed as she is dancing
This her dancing of intent
To the climax, culmination sans abillement
Now at last her dance is over
Arms outstretched they're in the clover.
In the verdant dappled light
Amid the grasses half her height.

# 09

## <u>Out Of Step</u>

Oh that they could only see us
The very fairies would be jealous
"Here I am my opal best
Am I not better than all the rest?
Look, am I lovely am I not?
Then why are you rooted to the spot?"
In her eyes once so compelling
Hero sees that tears are welling
He sees the hurt there in her face
At last leaps forward from his place.
But still he lacks the ardent verve
He dare not touch her swelling curve

"You, the dream I've craved all my life through
Now up here in the enchanted wood
My richest fantasy has come true.
If I'm looking pale or shy
You've put my head in a rainbow
And surely feel that I'll never die.
Here where the cuckoo calls across the wood
I fear I can't do what I should
Alas I can't perform this daring feat
To make this dream of mine complete."
Something gives him a little shove
He tastes the salts of her unrequited love
Then at a little distance stands
And cups her sweet face in his hands.
Kisses all her tears quite dry
"My angel, please don't cry

Oh Selsey I truly love you much
But you're far too wonderful to touch
And my mother always said to me
On your first date never let your passion free
Don't give yourself to me so lightly
You have a pretty hefty blighty.
I hate to see you so distressed
Let me help you to get dressed."
With many words he smoothes the damage done
And soon a little smile is won
With many soothing words again
To wash away her dreadful pain.
Soon poor Selsey's feeling fine
They stand together arms entwined.

# 10

## **Wanting Of Love**

"Oh Hero it's because I just adore you
And have such a passion for you
I'm no sterile pallid dove
I want red fire, I want love.
I have to love with all my might
This new passion I cannot fight
You've cut my very life in two
Before and after I met you.
And when I saw your rosy bower
I knew that I had climbed your tower
This state of mind there is no way round
My very heart for you is bound.
And from this point our love is growing
Now from this place we must be going."

Outside the wood it's warm and sunny
And both feel a little strange and funny
There's a mutual view in sight
And see each other in new light.
Now through the tollgate by the college
With the masters full of knowledge
For this is ever England after three
And surely it must be time for tea.
Stop for a moment by the pond
Look to the village there beyond
Famed for Dickens, Woodhouse, Thatcher
But I'm assured you'd never catch her.
And through the village slow their pace
For this is south London's finest place

Then hurry on there's one more find
That little Selsey has in mind.
They arrive there in a while
It must have been at least a mile.

# 11

## **The Brockwell Tea House**

This is Brockwell in the big house
The timeless tea house on the hill
Hot sausage rolls with mustard
Two apple pies and custard.
One more tea and as many cakes as they are able
Sitting at a small tin table
Now the clock tower reads after four
And the day holds just one thing more.
But in Hero's head there is mental strife
This joyous girl could be my wife
But how on earth could he cope?
Without a job there's just no hope.

"Now Selsey sweetheart you are my girl
But I have no one I can tell
How can I at least be bragging?
When I have this something nagging.
A secret inside my head does lurk
I've got to tell you I'm out of work."

"That's no worry," she says with a giggle
Then gives the strangest little wiggle.
"My uncle Albert works at Peckham Rye
I'll give him a bell it's worth a try
He's desperate for a gardening boy
But can't find a good one to employ.
If you know some Latin names
And have ambitions with higher aims
And you don't look like a yob

46

Albert I'm sure will give you a job."
"But Latin's for the learned
And I'm just not in that slot."
"Oh yes you are my sweetheart
We both speak it quite a lot.
Come let's go and I will show and tell."

There's an old kitchen garden
And ha ha! a real live wishing well
Once through the little iron gate
There's several paths that radiate.
And in between are beds of flowers
And here and there, clematis towers
Much better than the wishing well
And the fish pond in a dell.
The King of all garden trees
The one that bears the crimson mulberries
And a yew hedge archway like a tower
Climbing roses but not in flower
Seats where you may dream and potter
All enclosed by walls of faded terracotta.

Now Hero's head receives intrusion
She's naming plants in great profusion
"Now pay attention my little pet
Now listen to me and don't forget."

**12**

## Latin Roots

"Indigenous deciduous sound very much the same
So if you should mix them you wouldn't be to blame
Quercus is an oak tree with acorns plain to see
And Malus is apple that you could give to me.
Columinous Erectus is really just a pup
It means they're pretty straight or they're standing up
Prunus is a plum or a cherry tree
They're mostly grown for blossom and that confuses me.
Cardio is heart shaped, Folium a leaf
Flora is a flower, Parasitus is a thief
Back to this indigenous, that thing like you and me
A tree that is deciduous is not like a Christmas tree.
It's no use just knowing the way that things shoot
You have to know about their simple Latin root."

What a day I think they've won
Sit in the last rays of the dying sun
Soon the sun's below the wall
The garden then begins to cool.
They linger for a while, they both want to stay
The wall's still warm from that great day
Resting there they feel just fine
They gain the sun a second time.
Now they're running from the park
Or they'll be left there in the dark
A bus is waiting that will take them home
They run and run, and run some more
With a joy they never felt before.

The bus it makes its lurching ponderous way
Making others swerve and stray
For Selsey it's all been too much
She's soon asleep in Hero's clutch.
Here in his arms today
Yesterday a million miles away
But Hero's not quite as silly as he looks
For he has lots and lots of books.
And from the archives of his brain
Recalls the words with little strain
Birds of prey by T.F.Brown, page seven
To win the heart of a wild falcon
The bird must fall asleep on the trainer's arm
So it is with no small joy
He holds his new born precious toy.

# 13

## A Storm In His Arms

In his arms there is a space
That holds the perfection of her face
He gazes down with buoyant pleasure
Her natural beauty way out of measure.
Her Titian hair, its wild form
Like the leaves of autumn storm
Beneath the sleeping lashes lies
The magic emerald of her eyes.
Generous lips that smile with ease
Puffed as if been stung by bees
And the dearest little nose
Breathing there in sweet repose.
Eyebrows, their sweeping darkened line
"I bet she photographs divine."

Soon they're home and now it's twilight
Hero's bower still looks a delight
Now she stands there under the roses
Arms apart she pouts and poses.
Once there she takes her little chance
Gives a mocking song and dance
"Oh how I'd love a moment or two
Under this flowering rose arch with you.
If I came from a world without flowers
I would dance here for hours and hours
What heart could not return another day
Where June's roses bloom in May.
Now I must fly like a lark
Mum gets worried if I'm out after dark

Already she'll be fretting, you bet."
Click, click, click, and her diminishing silhouette.

"That girl is magic supersonic!
Plain for anyone to see
But have I done for her
What she has done for me?"

# 14

## Joy Of Living

He wakes to a day of bright elation
To an iridescent world of chromatic aberration
His body feels smooth and fast
And wonders how long this feeling will last.
This spring that bursts into a run
Today his life holds the essence of fun
And all the days that are to follow
Make all before seem dull and hollow.
Soon he's at the bus stop smiling
And as before she arrives beguiling
Greets him with a little wiggle
Lots of kisses and a giggle
Be at the hut there in the park
Albert Westward one o'clock sharp.

# 15

## <u>Jobs</u>

"Don't worry sweets when you start out
And you are without a single penny
For the roads that you can take
Are sweet and broad and many.
You could work as a grocer or a butcher
Or in the West End as a bespoke tailor
Maybe a builder or a plumber
But oh please not ever a sailor.
If you become a motor dealer
You will just keep winning
It's a perfect money maker
While all those wheels keep spinning.
Don't fret if your nose be big and your head be small
And your brain lacks ammunition
That's just fine, you'll be alright
You just become a politician."

Although midday is calm and warm
The sky is heavy with a storm
Then it suddenly starts to pelter
Hero runs like hell for shelter.
The rain keeps pouring for an hour
This isn't just a little shower
All about there's flashing lightening
Hero finds it a shade too frightening.
For the shelter he has found
Isn't really very sound
Heavy thunder shakes the park
And the sky is almost dark.

The rhododendrons where he cowers
Has become a dozen showers
Suddenly the rain it ceases
It's too late to straighten out his creases.
Although his appearance is quite shocking
He's soon at the hut door knocking
There is no answer so to the window has a peep
And sees old Albert fast asleep.
He stares at him for some while
What a tummy, what a pile!
Then suddenly he's awake and ready
Though his rolling gait's unsteady.
He looks at Hero with some alarm
"Blimey mate! That storm's done some 'arm
You look wetta than a waugha wat
Come inside, sit in my chair
By the electwic fire, and you git dwy
I've just gotta nip acwoss the woad
To the clock-ous like, for a quick one like
If the phone wings, say ees got cawt
In a wery evvy storm, oh yea!"

Now in the chair our Hero's splayed
He's just a little bit dismayed
This council job seems pretty good
The bosses chair before he should.
It's all so warm and comfy
But soon to fall like Humpty Dumpty
Oh that fire's warm and cosy
Soon his cheeks are going rosy.
Suddenly the door bursts open, with a crashing din
Reveals a fierce man's red face glaring in
"Och! In hells name who are you? One of Albert's mob?"
"No, no I've just come here to get a job."

"Albert Westward I bet he chose
Another sleeping partner I do suppose."
"Where's Westward," he's demanding
"Ees got cawt in a evvy storm
Well actually I mean I have a hunch
The rain has made him late for lunch."
The man is silent for a while
Then gives a little smirky smile
"So it's a job you want sonny, listen to me
Get in there and make me some tea
Then go outside and unload those rocks
All those sacks and that big box."
Hero makes the tea with great care
The fierce man sits in Albert's chair
Then outside he does his best
He thinks it must be some kind of test.
Groaning, heaving, growling, grunting
Pulling, twisting, panting, humping
That's all done without a rest
Still dressed in all his Sunday best.
Now he's looking very pleased
Even though he starts to wheeze
The fierce man he just drives off
Not a smile, not a word, but a cough.
So the fierce man's disappearing
Then Albert Westward reappearing
He's been standing behind a tree
So the fierce man couldn't see.
"That my good fwiend is Mr fierce face Fwyer.
Ee makes my ole life ewl, bweeding ewl.
I wouldn't mind but e don't know nuffin
about twees, e don't know nuffin abart flowers
or ow to gwow flowers. In fack, e is a
beliguwent, iwl mannered wiv a owwibawl tempa

and is ead is fawl up wiv igowance. And wot is more, if the union could see wot e's just dun wiv you, wewll, they would be bweeding confounded oh yer. Now you ava walk rand the park and meet the uvvers then come back 'ere at fwee o'clock."

# 16

## Peckham Park

Now our Hero's taken by surprise
The park around him seems twice alive
Warm breezes blow the clouds away
This is the wonderful fifth of May.
A flowering sun is out and beaming
Makes the park a jungle steaming
Mass tulips in their sodden beds
Pink Rhododendrons lolling heads.
Clematis climbers strung with glory
Burst with incandescent fury
Then a bridge, the sweetest little waterfall
Thrushes splashing tuneful call.
The keeper dreams by his bowling green
A greener green as ever was seen
Gazes at his emerald table
He's done as much as he is able.
For he always tries his best
Now the rain can do the rest
Round the duck pond as in every park
A must for mothers, children and dogs that bark.
Squawking mallards, darting coots
Busy in the reeds and shoots
A swan nests on an island, built on a motor tyre
With a countenance as fierce as Fryer.
She's out of reach and out of sight
From foxes lethal prowling night
In the woods a rushing tributary
With wild flowers bright and many.
This little river feeds the pond

Then disappears somewhere beyond
Dives below, beneath the deck
To meet the ancient river Peck.
And in the ageing arboretum
A bright flaming red Palmatium
Up in the trees a constant song
Both short, sharp, clear and strong.
Song sweet as to infinity
And even crows to aid the symphony
In his mind the music lingers there
For some time after it has left the air.
Back at the hut it's almost three
And there is Albert with some tea
A bun for you, a bun for me
A tea for you and the same for me
Albert starts, no time for answers.

"Did you meet the gewls in the garden?
The bestest workers I av ever come acwoss,
and contwy to common belief they don't
never stop for a chat, don't never stop
for a fag, an wot is more, they are tough
as bweeding oxes, oh yer. They are uttaly
bweeding wonderful, an wivout em we'd
all be workin our guts out, and thass a fack!"

"It's a wewl known secwet that awl carncil
workers are daft, stoopid and igowant, but
wot is worse, bwoody minded. But not them
gewls, they're weal gooduns, oh yer. Now I'm
wery pleased to tewl you, that you av got the
job and started at eight this morning, if you
get me meaning like. Now off you go, your
sweetart is coming to meet you, and I don't want

er awound ear upsettin the boys. She is a wery
pwecoshus an pwetty gewl, and that is for
sure. But it beats me where she git er good
looks fwom. All that side of the family are as
ugally as edgeoggs an just abart as pwickly,
oh yer. 'Ere, just before you go, I want you to
look at this. It's my libawy for when it's dinner
time, or it's waining and we aint got much to
do like. Then we can av a littawl wead and git
some culcha wot is sadly lacking these days
wiv awl this wowdy music in their eds. Look
'ere, The Life and Times of Queen Victorwia,
Darwin and the Beagle, Nelson's battles, the
Vintage motorcar by Clutton and Stanford an
undreds of uvvers. There aint no book 'ere that
is salacious and wulga or don't do no
betterment to your ed after you av wead it an
thass a fack!"

From the shady park he's running
Across a sun drenched Rye all steaming
His heart is racing his feet are flying
Over grass, damp as the breast of woman's crying.
Then hears whispers of his mother
"Of course you're as good as any other
Don't stay forever in that pit."
"Go on Hero I knew you'd do it."
Sees his love, a distant splash of colour
And he knows that it can be no other
With birdsong in his ears still ringing
Oh what glorious love of living.
Then feels more fire in his pace
And quickly wiping out that space
At last he feels he's really got her

His life is now phantasmagoria.
Grabs poor Selsey by her waist
And throws her squawking into space
While still floating in the air
Angels catch her if you dare.
By her hands swings her up and round
Then lays her dizzy on the ground
And madly kisses her smiling face
Still flushed from being up in space.
Tells her how his heart's a-stir
That he wants much more of her
And that she's his very life and limb
And strange things she's done for him.

# 17

## Loves Madness

"This madness in my heart
That didn't ought to be
Such yearning here inside
That never used to be.

With this madness in my heart
There's nothing I can do
This burning here within
The flames are all for you.

If you had a change of heart
Or we should ever part
No other girl could ever quench
This madness in my heart."

# 18

## Exotic Joys

"Oh Hero you're not like other boys
You bring me such exotic joys
Feelings I just can't explain
A sort of pleasant flowing pain.
You give me such a vibrant ache
Now half the night I lay awake
There's no more darkness in my head
When I'm laying in my bed.
The nights are full of pearls, it seems
And you are forever present in my dreams
I often dream that we have wings
And ride the storms of Saturn's rings.
That seems way out for sure
But truth be known I dream much more
My tethered soul, you set it free
With pretty things you say to me.
And when I hear such words from you
You get my tummy jumping too
My foggy head fills with expectation
My body zings with magic elation
There's nothing I'll not do
To change my ways, myself for you."

"No please don't ever rearrange
You don't ever have to change
Just promise you will never stray
And be just as you are today.
But don't you ever leave me
Please never to deceive me

You may feel like a tiny seedling
But to me you are a tree
It's impossible to thank you
For the things you have done for me.
We used to be just ones
And now we are worth two
And you will never know
Of just how I think of you."

**19**

## My Honey Bee

"You're like eating bread and butter
While laying in the hay
You are my new born flower
My honey bee in May.
You charm me just like music
On a balmy summer day
You're my flashy little sports car
I want to drive away.
You're my sugar of entice
My sweet bird of paradise
And when I kiss your swollen lips
You are my plate of fish and chips.
You have always been so close
Yet out of reach so far
Oh how I want to love you
Just the way you are."

Selsey's rising from the grass
Makes a little mocking pass
Kneeling as if about to pray
"Yes I promise I won't stray.
Hands together and very still
I promise that I never will
But as yet I haven't got a thing
Where is this little golden ring?
What is love and what is gold?"
They have a gypsy love of old
So in love and homeward bound
Both their arms around around.

Through the turnings pitter patter
Unaware of London's clatter
Soon in his garden full of trees
Buddleia, butterflies and busy bees
Sipping ice drinks on a chair
Soaking up the sun and air.

## 20

### Dare I Dream

"In my dreams and in my head
I see you clean the house and make the bed
I hear you singing in the bath
I see you sitting by the hearth.
Another dream but I don't know if I should
You're in the kitchen where my mother stood
One day my angel, you'll eventually be mine
And our two lives will close entwine.
In my dreams and in my head
Dare I see you close to me in bed."

"All those dreams I want to share
But as things are I cannot dare
Oh Hero if you only knew
With how I struggle with what to do.
For something bars the road for us
As tall and as wide as a London bus
Mum's nerves and heart are very poorly
It makes me sad, I feel it sorely.
I have no sisters or a brother
And she is my only sweet loving mother
So I can't forsake her for a lover
Not for you or any other.
Now I have fallen, I'm here in your trap
But never really planned for that
All my troubles have been told
Our rosy future must go on hold."

"Leave your mother, don't you ever
That's not right or very clever
To split you from your mum, no never
Because for you, I'll wait forever.
We can be as happy as two mice
In our prefabricated tryst
And Miss Carnival, what is more
We have red roses over the door.
So call as often as you may
Just any time of the night or day."
"Yes on Wednesday that's for sure
I'll be here knocking on your door
Now Hero I must be going
Mum said the lawn needs mowing."
And it's clickety click click click
And her diminishing silhouette.

On Wednesday all things were right
But of Selsey there's no sound or sight
Staring at the box that horrid black and white
"I suppose it's bed, alas it is goodnight
Oh Selsey Carnival what shall I do?
I've lost my heart to you and I thought you loved me
too
I suppose it was a thing for a little while
And me I was no match for her oblivious style."
Thursday things were just the same
On Friday it's desperation and it begins to rain
Staring from the window at the lamp light in the dark
He has a gloomy feeling of doubt and losing heart.

# 21

## Gone With The Rain

"Little windswept raindrops
By the lamplight glow
They sparkle for a moment
Then into darkness go.
They remind me of dear Selsey
The sweetest girl I know
We walked beneath the lamplight
But then she had to go.
Why did she not believe me
When I love her so
Maybe she has another
That she can keep in tow
And she is like the raindrops
That sparkle then they go."

Saturday morning holds no glory
Hero's feeling sick and poorly
Up and early out of bed
Runs from the house that's like a shed.
At the bus stop, no one's there
He's just waiting in despair
Buses come and buses go
But no sign of Selsey's bow.
That's the flowing muslin bow
To keep her crazy hair in tow
So to the park, but things are dire
By the shed he's faced by Fryer.

"What are you doing here on Saturday laddy?
Westward booked you in for overtime no doubt."
"No sir, just come for a walk." "Och, a walk, anyone
who has time for a walk at this hour is either mad
or has nothing better to do! Now listen to me laddy
If you would care for a wee bit of overtime, see
that long walk there, I want every weed and last
blade of grass removed. Here's a knife, but before
you start make me a good strong cup of tea. Now
get cracking laddy, you're on time and a half."

On his hands and knees it isn't much fun
It's cold, drafty and a long way from the sun
With the knife and a little spade
He takes two hours to leave the shade.
Then an hour out beneath the sun
And that is even less like fun
His hands are sore, his head is spinning
Now his eyes see things are dimming.
And the lines in front are wavy
No wonder they call this paving crazy
Sees a shadow dancing from the air
Feels that someone's standing there.

"At last, I've looked for you all over
And here you are with weeds and clover
Why are you working out of hours?
I want the weekend to be ours!"

"Well on Wednesday night you didn't come
I thought you had gone forever."
"How could you doubt me so?
Me? Gone forever? Never, never, never
My feelings now you surely know

My love for you it isn't shy
Forever, that's no trivial game
I want you forever, do you think I lie?
Poor mum she's been in hospital
What's more, in intensive care!
And I couldn't possibly leave her
When her poor heart it needs repair.
They say she needs a new valve
And more likely to need two
And all the time you're thinking
It's my heart that isn't true
Oh Johnny how could you doubt me!"
And to our Hero's great surprise
She puts her arms around him
And cries and cries and cries.

**22**

## <u>My Racing Heart</u>

"It's this elusive chasm
Here inside my heart
That is completely empty
Whenever we're apart.

You're waiting at the bus stop
There's that pleasant refrain
Your arms out to hold me
And you call out my name.

I tremble, I'm breathless
My racing heart to beat
I feel a trifle dizzy
The very instant that we meet.

There's a spring in my step.
A twinkle in my eye
A smile on my lips
That cannot tell a lie.

There's adrenalin rushing
My fuel out of sight
I have the touch paper
Only you can ignite.

It's your magic, your spark
My bosom swells to a flame
Sadly to burn out
Until I'm with you again."

So off to the café to have a little lunch
But by the time they come back
She's her usual honeybunch.
"Now I want to get this job done
Because I'm in a rush
You'll have to get two draw hoes
And then find a besom brush.
You've been working with a bread knife
And it makes you look a fool
This job it can't be finished
Unless you have the proper tool."

So they work away the long walk
Much faster than they should
It isn't even three o'clock
And it's done and looking good.
No sooner have they cleared away
An apparition they can see
Fryer's marching up the long walk
No doubt he wants some tea.
He isn't looking very fierce
In fact it's nothing like that
He wears a silly smile
Much like an Easter hat.
"Ah what have we here laddy, a wee piece
of free labour I see."
"Oh no, I er, this is Sel."
"Och I know who she is, a man would have
to be blind or stupid to miss a fine wee lass
like Selsey, and just look at that long walk,
it's never looked better. She's put a woman's
touch to that for sure. Why this Selsey is the
original Blythen Bonny."
"Don't you mean Bonny and Clyde?"

Mister Fryer laughs, "This wee friend of yours Selsey,
he could do himself a favour going
on the stage with a wee droll sense of humour he
has." Suddenly our Mr Fryer seems stuck for words
to say. "I was er, just wondering laddy...er if he could
make you a wee cup of tea."
"Well he can't he isn't really free, but come down to the
hut with me."
"Och, I'll make yee a wee strong cup of tea." But Fryer's
not at all put out, he's quite smitten by her clout.

With Selsey now exuding charm
Off down the long walk arm in arm
Hero's amazed, it's stunned his fragile mind
Carrying the tools, he comes trailing on behind
But there's a little more in store
The chatter even shocks him more.

"Och at Chelsea I only pick up a silver. But
would you believe it, at Wisely I won a wee gold.
Those California Camellias just simply knocked
them out."
"Not bad Mr Fryer, that is for someone who don't know
nothing about flowers or growing flowers."
"Och, don't be too hard on your uncle he's not a bad
fellow. So long as you can keep him
awake, and he's a very ill man as you know. Oh yes!"

So you see where flowers grow in earth
It follows there is often mirth
So after tea they were both sent home
Across the sunny Rye to roam
Now he has her by herself
With kisses thanks her for her stealth.

## 23

## <u>Good Light</u>

"I was in such an awful plight
Yet you soon put me in good light
With your smile, your inimitable style
You bring good light around, around
You bring good light around me.
Just no one can resist your smile
No one can scarcely match your guile
Whenever you are close to me
My happiness abounds, astounds
You bring such joy around me."

And so it was through their first spring
Just each other, they have everything
Endless walks and weekend play
Both happy in their working day.

**24**

## English Summer

It's wonderful in England
Now that summer's here
The swallows fly past Italy
To be here every year!
That contrary little turncoat
The month that we call May
Can be as good as paradise
Or a savage winter's day.
Sweet June dressed in long days
Her hot colours take us by surprise
After that intermittent spring
So often spiced with lies
If you choose to get up early
The sun's already high
Shining through your windows
From a placid pastel sky.
It's climbing the tall day
Scribes a never ending arc
The afterglow at midnight
Still rivalling the dark.
Scorpio with her red star
Brightly sparkles in the glow
I think it's worth a look
Ask someone in the know.
When the old day lays dying
A new infant's being born
A warm ephemeral night
Soon blown away by dawn.
The natives they get restless

And go rushing to the sea
Clothed in ghastly attire
It's an awful thing to see.
Such visual atrocities
They reappear each year
Worse than comic postcards
They sell there at the pier.
When the mercury is over 80°f
They call that a wave
So don't go off to southern climbs
Just think of the money you'll save.

In the heat our Hero's sighing
Selsey thinks her mum is dying
Today she has an operation
Both their brains in dislocation.
Every night she isn't there
He walks the hill to stand and stare
Across all London's hazy glare.
On the fifth night deep in thought
His poor mind a shade distraught
By himself just standing there
He offers up a little prayer.

"I've loved her since that first glance
And know there'll be a time for us
A seed born on the wind of chance.
I have it here within me
Like a tender note of music
With impending symphony.
I guard it as if it were a child
Lest my passion may suppress
This growing flower of our love
My all my very happiness.

Her dream is always with me
Now in my drowsy night
That sunny dream draws closer
Into the shadow of my solitude.
Now with fresh hope I stare
Where the great lights
Touch the distant city glare
Happy to sleep, but eager for dawn.
Knowing somewhere she is there
Please God, make a time for us
That is my only prayer."

It's wonderful how those upstairs
Can quickly answer fervent prayers
While Hero's fast asleep and rocking
There's a desperate Selsey loudly knocking.
Now Hero's up and hurried dressing
Selsey at the doorbell pressing
He with shrill bells in his ears
She poor girl is close to tears.

# 25

## Saturday

Now Saturday's a funny day
Just a slip can change your way
Back and forth to work each day
Chained to your job, safe you'll stay.
Yes Saturday's a dangerous time
Your life can blow up like a mine
A day that can upset your life
Can bring you sorrow, joy or strife.
Could be the day you wed or tether
And change your bloody life forever.

Let in at last, she stumbles through the door
Quickly scooped up before she hits the floor.
"You're looking troubled you really are
First time I've caught a falling star
And you just got me out of bed
Not the worst news ever, is your mother dead?"
"Oh no, she's had her operation
It's miraculous, she's really doing fine
It isn't my mum, the trouble is all mine
Now she's feeling so much better
She's never coming back
She will be living with her sister
Off the beaten track.
She said that her poor heart
Is because she's always lived in towns
Now she wants whole food and exercise
And go walking on the Downs.
Her sister lives near Selsey

That's the place where I was born
It's very bright and sunny and often very warm.
But the trouble is our landlord
Cannot make enough to pay his tax
He wants to cut the house up
And make it into several flats.
I can't afford one, I can't get a loan
So it won't be very long now
That I'll be out of house and home."
"Well my pretty angel, the news is very sad
Now let's have some tea and toast
Then things won't seem so bad."

After breakfast things are smooth
His kindly words, her troubles soothe
With different eyes she sees his prefab
Maybe after all it's not that bad.
Flat roofs they draw the sun a lot
By noon it's getting stuffy hot
Outside the garden calls
Now on a pile of straw she sprawls.
Stripped down to her underwear
She's looking pink and delightfully bare
Soon he's outside to have a peep
"That hay was to activate my compost heap."
She doesn't answer, her brain is numb
Dulled by the pleasures of the blazing sun
Whenever she lays down and goes to bed
All sorts of things flash bright in her head.
Mostly they're good but sometimes they're dread
But oh how they roll about in her head.

## 26

### To Wilt And Laze

"My glorious golden midsummer day
Half drugged I lay here in the hay
And feel warm thermals over me
Blow more hot winds from over the sea.
I need another thirty days like this
To scorch the seaside towns to bliss
And in the fields that lay beyond
Turn the wheat heads brassy blonde.
Green apples in the orchard now
Blush pink and sweeten on the bough
And with this heated air divine
Turn the hops brown on the vine.
Please my tomatoes by the wall
Be kissed by sun, grow fruity tall
And in the thirty days to come
Bleach my hair and tan my tum.
Oh it's wonderful to wilt and laze
Heavenly English summer days."

Sometime later he's cooking in the kitchen
She comes from the garden rushing, screaming
Outside sudden rain is teaming.
Great drops all sploshy warm
Just what's left of a burnt out storm
As quickly it's come it's gone.
The sun now back and burning strong
The garden shed is red like rust
Don't be alarmed it's desert dust.

**27**

## Heat Wave

Sing, oh sing great winds from Africa
Music from your dark romantic heart
Blow, blow Sahara's burning sands
Across Spain's sweltering hinterland.
The Pyrenees shall not cool your ardour
With your sweeping thermal hand
Caress our cool shores to blissful blue
And wash all England's fields and farms
With your pink tears of summer joy.
For a while this greenhouse island
Shall dull the brain to walking pace
Only the swifts with their titanic zeal
Rush wilfully like demented children
Screaming and dancing in our happy sky
Their scimitar wings cutting the torpid air.
Rejoice brief summer's here again
Sweet scent of cut grass and lolling flowers
The drone of bees, the shade of trees
Long listless days of pleasant idleness.
Drowsy afternoons of garden paradise
And airless nights of heated blood
Sing, sing on great winds of Africa.

Yes, Saturday really is a funny day
She's left her troubles in the hay
They're eating kippers and crusty bread
All worries vanish from her head
"Hero, is that cream cake all for me?
It is, then I'll have another cup of tea.

"I've got a picnic already made
We'll find a nice place in the shade
But we'll see your uncle, you never know
He may have some place you can go.
But at the park things are bad
Poor Albert's close to fighting mad
He looks quite ill and full of woe
Off he goes, no How do you do, or Hello."

"I've 'ad a bweeding 'owwible day. Last night there
was a bweak in. The p'lice 'av bin dann ere awl morning
making a list of the damage done an' the stuff wot 'as
bin taken. Johnny Wesley 'as kiwlled one of them
ornimental ducks. I'd like to bwain the litawl owwa,
and
it's got so 'ot I can't 'ardly fink or bweeve pwoper. I've
been up an' bweeding dan, in an bweeding art, up an
bweeding dan, in an bweeding art awl bweeding day
long.

"An' as you do know, I am a wery iwl man, oh yer."

"Mr Westward I'll make you a nice cup of tea
And you can have one of our sandwiches."
"That would be wery welcome, wery welcome
That is wery kind of you indeed
Wery kind of you both, oh yer."

Now they're walking in the street
Paving stones do scorch their feet
Passing by the cemetery wall
They both think in there it does look cool
To have a picnic in there's off beat
The trees the grass would soothe our feet

But for some reason, God only knows
There is a notice
"From Friday the 20th this cemetery will be closed."
Hero sighs, "All those trees all that shade
In there we'd really have it made."
"Don't worry darling, have no fear
Your clever little Selsey's here."
Soon through a gap there in the wall
Where Russian vine hangs there like a shawl
Into a cool green world, city of the dead
The sight before them turns Hero's head.

**28**

## City Of The Dead

Graves and crosses, tombs and temples
In every shape and myriad samples
Angels kneeling and angels crying
By the tombs, there's angels lying.
Angels with their wings outspread
Lost in the green above their head
Here and there a little space
Where the sun can show its face.
But mostly things cannot be seen
They lay behind a leafy screen
Ivy covers most the ground
With little footpaths through and round.
By the graves, the paths are turning
Over thousands not returning
In silence bare their rude intrusion
Beneath the stones in great profusion
They rush by in youthful folly
And desecrate death's dark melancholy.

On one large stone there is an inscription
In loving memory of Elisabeth Rosini Foggo
Who departed this life aged 89;
In the year of our Lord 1883
On the 25th day of December
Here lyeth seven of her twelve children
Who died in infancy;
Emma Rose aged 6 months
Poppy May aged 5 weeks
John William aged 3 days

William John aged 18 months
Sally Polly aged 2 and a half years
Peter George aged 2 months
Alexia Vivian aged 4 weeks.

Selsey's going at some pace
She knows a magic, secret place
Over fallen graves in awful shambles
Under branches hung with brambles
Twisting turning on untrod paths
Sesley stops, they've arrived at last.

**29**

## In Soft Summer Air

"This lovely place I've found for you
All alone there's just us two
It's a perfect Eden, we have won
I can't think of a better one.
All this grass so soft and lush
Just listen to that deadly hush
No sounds can penetrate the trees
Just us and a few old bumble bees.
We could be the children of that first garden
I'm quite sure God would give us pardon
Be just the same as they if we dare
And bathe in the sweet soft summer air."

Already her poor stomach's churning
But not for love, it's food she's yearning
So under the shade of a towering tree
There in peace they have some of their tea.
Then in each other's arms they lay
And doze the afternoon and more away
Suddenly they awake lost to all sense of time
In the sky a great moon is floating
Through distant clouds of rosy wine.
In their little private clearing
Where all sun's rays fast disappearing
A grave close by without a head
Just flat and as large as a double bed.
It's a mighty piece of paving
Moss grows deeply over its engraving
All day it has been baked in the sun

A perfect place for impending fun.
Sesley knows she's come of age
And sees this as her rightful stage
"Give me that last glass of wine
I'll toast all those beneath, gone is their time
Tonight this stage is mine, mine, mine!
And with one tip I'll drink this wine."
She kicks her flip-flops in the air
And stands on the stone, her feet are bare
Feels warmth rising from the stone
This is her time, her life to own.
Her arms outspread stands for a while
Then spins round and round in crucifixal style
Throws the wine glass in the air
And where it falls, she couldn't care.
Tugs the buttons of her summer dress
And casts it down, it lays there in a mess
And all restricting lingerie is cast away
Abandoned, lays about in disarray.
"Oh Hero, I've such a passion for you
This be my hallmark, my love is true
There's nothing more to show
No more I can say, no other place to go.
There's nothing more that I can do
To prove this love I have for you
Now I show you all my treasures
With you alone, I'll share my pleasures.
My virgin body here for you
Everything will be brand new
Though the night be short, it shall be sweet
I feel strange music in my feet
I must dance without a tune
I will to the beat of a sailing moon."

# 30

## In The Crimson

As the moon there slowly rises
Her little love dance has no disguises
Moonlight on her bosom dancing
In harmony with her swaying prancing.
"Oh Hero where do you lay my sweet
Don't hide yourself from love and fun
You have to make the quantum leap
Or all your words of love are cheap."
From the shadows of the night
Our hero sees this scary sight
But his love for her is always thirsting
Now his unicorn is rising bursting.
Sees her glowing thighs her Venus hiding
He knows that he must soon be there abiding
This crimson night so full of beauty
"Go on Hero, it's time to do your duty."
In a moment they are as one
Lost to thrills of new born fun
Their vital organs are colliding
With exquisite slipping sliding.
In her brain great wheels revolve
As scrumptious secrets there unfold
In her heart there's fervent loving
"Take my cup of molten gold
With your flaming sword of old."
In her cauldron alloys are burning
As she satisfies her yearning
All the time she's swooning, sighing
Sings a song that sounds like crying.

And as her song with climbing height
Comes high C with purple flashing light
Cataclysmica delight.
Now in her eyes the stars are falling
As she feels her passions cooling
The raging storm at last subside
Comes gentle waves this is low tide
Such ecstasies they cannot last
And all too soon they're in the past.

"Hero that was to me the sweetest song
My aunt said that all things like that were wrong
You turned my poor body into fire
Oh that woman's such a liar!
I think we've crossed an ocean wide
But I'm feeling sort of sad inside
I could go on and never tire
But for all the ashes of the fire.
You ignite the fire, that's just the start
I have a little restless angel in my heart
For when we stopped I felt a pain
So can we do it all again?"
I'm afraid to tell you that he did
Yes exactly as she bid
So quickly returned to their erotic abandon
Wanton and careless of where it will land them.
And there they are all spent of ardour
Now empty of their fruitful larder
So on their mossy bed they lay
Until shaken by the break of day.

# 31

## <u>Smouldering Night</u>

"Your arms are around me still sweaty and hot
This moss covered stone is our nuptial cot
Your eyes are dilated and smouldering light
A glow in our fleeting midsummer night.
Your face without motion, still warm from our love
I wonder if our sins are blessed from above
Consummation has bound us, oh ever so strong
Silence together be our true lovers song.
Words said in churches are clumsy and dread
Soon sadly forgotten or fall out of bed
It's almost tomorrow, not a star left to shine
My hopes for tomorrow, is that you'll always be mine.
As I lay by your body divine in its form
My prayer is a life with you, a time without storm."

**32**

## A New Day

"The sky grows brighter, beckons the sun
Brings a new life for us, exciting and fun
Rise from the shadows to the half light of dawn
Get up with me, run with me, our new life is born."
So they run with a fury of wild abandon
It would take a gazelle I'm sure to outrun them
Through leaf covered twigs and dew covered grasses
You wouldn't need specs to see their two arses.
Then in the end all horse power gone
Go back to silence the sweets lovers song
Pick up their pieces and steal away home
Selsey she whispers "I can't find my comb."
Through shadowy streets, how naughty they've been
With an odd feeling they shouldn't be seen
Silent and empty the spooky old road
Secretly, stealthily, step inside his abode.
Once inside they make for the bed
And instantly sleeping as if they were dead
He is her Adam and she is his Eve
And I can assure you she's not going to leave!

Selsey's deep in sleep and dreaming
She's all alone and in the clearing
In her dreaming eyes she sees
Angels standing amid the trees
Sees her aunty by the grave
"Oh my girl, you're too late to save."
Then strange people dressed in shrouds
Coming through in waves and crowds

In her ears the angels sing
"Where on earth's your golden ring?"
Is this hell, no it is heaven
She's wide awake it's past eleven
Up she gets and makes some tea
But feels a strange anxiety.
While Selsey frets about her rings
Hero dreams of far different things
It's a good thing Hero's dreams aren't real
To say the least, they are quite surreal.
He's on a horse and clothed in armour
And feeling he's a mighty charmer
Riding round the open clearing.
Pretty girls on all sides cheering
He's got one with such great ease
Another two would be a breeze
Who wants marriage and golden rings
And all the other silly things.
Now I'm having all this fun
"Sesley does" the angels answer him as one
But all at once he's thrown in the air
The horse cries out in shocked despair.
Poor animal he's trodden on Selsey's glass
And Hero's crashed down on the grass
But hears a voice from up above
Much like the cooing of a dove.
"Oh wake to a golden morn my love
Wash sandy sleep from thine eyes
Rise from your perfumed bed my love
You have missed a great sunrise."

"Wake up sweety it's late in the day
I've got a lot of things to say
Sit you up and drink this tea

And while you do you can listen to me.
It's a pretty nervy thing stepping out with you
I have this sinking feeling, I don't know what to do
Suddenly my blue skies, have sadly all turned grey
Something seems to tell me I ought to run away.
It is this little something I really can't define
Just what is yours and is there anything that's mine?
There's this melancholy feeling deep down in my tum
I think I must be missing my darling little mum
If my skies turn grey I won't really run away
But hopefully you'll sympathise and listen when I say
Will you always have that loving touch?
It's the little things that mean so much
Blow me a kiss when you say goodbye
And use kind words that make me cry.
The sort that make me walk tall
And be there to catch me if I fall
Will you cuddle me when I'm sad
And forgive me when I'm bad.
When I'm feeling down and want to cry
Just be sweet and don't ask why
And if you ever see me in despair
Just run your fingers through my hair.
The sort of things my mum would do
Her love for me was always true
Tell me can I live right here with you?
Are we going to marry too?
Will you buy me a ring of gold
And love me now, and when I'm old?"

"Oh Selsey to leave you without a ring
Why I'd never dream of such a thing
In fact I have a ring right here
It's been waiting here for many a year.

In this little box beneath my bed
Collecting dust since my mother was dead
It belonged to her and her mother before
Very precious I can say no more."
As the box is opened her words go into stall
A long long silence, "Oh it's beautiful."
A wonderful ruby the shape of a heart
To keep two sparkling diamonds apart
Surrounded all by tiny pearls
Just the ring for romantic girls
It's an antique of course and very old
And as requested is hallmarked gold.

"Oh Hero how you do my bidding
I really thought that you were kidding
It is a gem with splendour way above
And look it fits me like a glove.
Be sure I'll guard it covetously
But I think it's much too good for me
Only on Sunday I'll wear such a thing
I'll be happy all week with a curtain ring.
Well it's Sunday today and I shall wear it
And we shall delight in its glory and glit
In front of your cheval I'll pose
Be dazzled by its sparkles and glows
Between my breasts it really looks good
Or on my purse but I don't think I should."
For some time by the mirror she's posing and talking
And acting, dancing and swaying, cavorting
Fingers are spread in the form of a fan
Vibrating her fingers as fast as she can.
"Oh no Sir I'm sorry I've been dancing a lot
And I'm really rather terribly hot
Dancing as couples makes me feel in a cage

I'm far better a solo, you know on the stage."
As Hero watches his temperature rises
Now Selsey is in for more pleasant surprises
As he picks her up there's red blood in his head
And lustfully kissing puts her back in the bed.
"Now listen to me you dizzy old head
It's already too long since you've been out of this bed
But I love your mime and silly old tricks
You're full of surprises my sweet pick'n'mix.
If you take this ring and marry me
I'm never going to set you free
The new law is and it will have to do
You are mine and everything else belongs to you.
So come fly to me my sweet
And run with singing angels feet
My hot little dolly sweet meat
You're surely good enough to eat."

Now we must move on ahead
And leave them to their joyous bed.

**33**

## Another Safety Pin

Spring is here it's Saturday morning
Ominous clouds are up there yawning
Selsey's pregnant but no one knows
But she worries that it shows.
She's standing under Hero's bower
Oh God, there is another shower
She looks resplendent and well she may
It is her much awaited wedding day.
She's all in white Edwardian style
That glorious hair up in a pile
Tiny waist all tucked and towed in
Her bosom slightly overflowing
And on the chain around her neck
Hangs a little cross of Witby jet
Her aunt said it's very unlucky
And will bring her hard work and tragedy
But Selsey couldn't give a care
What is life if it isn't a dare.
She's defiant, splendid and believe it or not
She bought her outfit in a charity shop
Cash in hand her head's in no whirl
Economy yes I like that in a girl.
Selsey doesn't need expensive tags
She'd still look good if dressed in rags
Her mother's calling, "Please come in
I've found another safety pin."
But the wedding car comes lurching, breaking
Over dreadful humps of council making
A vintage Austin heavy twelve four

For a wedding you could ask no more
Plate glass windows two feet high
That puts the bride up in the sky.

By the church the birds are singing
Up in the tower bells are ringing
Though the sun is in for a try
Great white clouds are rushing by.
Now Selsey in the car appears
Growling in its lower gears
To her it's all an added thrill
An antique car, Victorian church upon a hill.
Guests assemble in their pews
With fancy hats and polished shoes
Organ thunders here comes the bride
Makes her feel she wants to hide.
Admiring coos from all sides
In no time that dreadful feeling dies
But all the same her heart is fluttering
Hears her aunt beside her muttering
She really wanted Albert to give her away
But listen to what he had to say.

"No! A wedding is the first day of a bweeding
cerlamity an' always ends in tears and I don't
wanna be no par' of it. An' some more advice
to finish it, listen 'ere Johnny and don't fagit.
Don't never put your wife on a pedestawl she will
soon fagit oo put er up there. An' anyow she
won't fiwl safe so 'igh up an' soon start actin'
strange in many ways an' automately become a
worry an' an embarrassment to everyone
oh yeah and thass a fack!!
And another fing, don't let that gewl

outta sight for long. A lotta men live
in a sexual desert an if they see
some fwoot they wiwl make a gwab
at it, even if it is covered wiv
pwikawls. Oh yer."

The vicar dressed in black and white
Smiles down politely from his awesome height
Hero comes down the aisle to bat
Wears a pea green suit and a pink top hat.
He looks a neddy and he knows it
But his mother-in-law, she chose it
So he soldiers on what can he do?
She paid the hire charges too.

"John Hero Smith will you take Selsey Carnival Franklin
To be your lawful wedded," etc etc.
In the end they both said "I will."
It's sealed with a kiss and an ummm and a purr
Then along through an arch to the register
Selsey signs with a flourishing style
Then taken away by friends for awhile
But Hero is faced by a man in grey
His compelling eyes now bar his way.

"Be careful my dear boy, marriage is not such
a happy affair as it appears at weddings. It
is for strong men, the reason being if you
don't hold it together every day of the year
it simply falls apart, and that my dear boy is
divorce, in divorce you have no rights. No right
over your house, no right over your children
and little or no right over your money. The lady
for some unfathomable reason holds all five aces.

You may think there aren't five aces in the pack
but in divorce there are, you should be told.
Just sign here please."

Hero is shaken and his signature too
It's too late now, it'll have to do
He goes looking for Selsey his eyes full of strife
But nobody notices, they look at his wife.
It's the day of her life and she looks so endearing
But sleet and wind greet her appearing
But she makes not the slightest fuss
She just smiles profusely and looks luminous.

**34**

## Aunt Eadie's Hat

Such a precarious game to play
That springtime wedding day
Rogue winds can lift the wedding dress
And cast the veil down in a mess.
Aunt Eadie's hat she had to hire
Found two weeks later in a mire
The marquee taken by a sudden squall
Gone the wedding cake and all.
A photo just the groom and bride
The rest have found somewhere to hide
Another freezing torrent of rain
To wash confetti down the drain
All plans and money to pay
The weather can leave all in disarray.

But they haven't booked a grassy ramble
May the 10th they take no gamble
The Rivoli Ballroom Crofton Park
It's rather swish bejewelled and dark.
The owner is a friend of our bride
So takes the table with some pride
Except for Hero's broken spell
The reception all goes pretty well.
Everyone is there that ought to be
Sans Albert and Miss E Rigby
Hero's called upon to make a speech
Still stunned and words seem out of reach.
Feeling he has been left in the lurch
After his encounter in the church
Although he starts somewhat shakily
He then steels himself defiantly.

## 35

## <u>My Bride Divine</u>

"Love like other words with four letters
That are used far too often by my uppers and betters
And I'm told by my peers who are wiser than me
Love's a word that's been stolen and should be set free.
Taken by new ones that have whisked it away
And applied it to floosies that don't last a day
That love is not for little girls
With their deceitful smiles and winning curls.
Real love they say is for your classic car
Or perhaps your favourite sporting star
Real passions are for football games
The winning goal and far flung aims.
And for all the other sports of old
Like running for Olympic gold
Well ladies and gentlemen, if I be true
Sure I'll have to disappoint you.
I cannot bite the edges of the pie
Selsey, she will be my centre 'til I die
Worth far more than gold or treasures
She is my variety of pleasures.
So real love is for my bride divine
For with her I wake to days that shine
It's simple, I love her and the world is mine."

Selsey laughs and rocks with joy
"That's my Hero that's my boy."
Her mother just beams with pride
And of course her Aunty cried.

# 36

## A Sonnet For The Bride

In joyous and proud countenance stand
Fresh from the alter flush in glorious resplendence
With veil sailing and garland to hand.
Spring from your Madonna years into your April days
Come bite deep while fruits are sweet to taste
While limbs are supple and easy
Run wild then but not with too much haste
Yet be careful but not too wise.
Alter not for things that may be, time will care for time
Be true to your bosom and cultivate charm
For these are possessions that intoxicate as wine.
What value a briar without a smiling rose?
Be merry and store much glee and good heart
That in your fruitful years you shall not part.

Then time just flies and all too soon
They're off to Cornwall for a honeymoon
A brief two weeks they go to stay
To a secret place that's far away.
To an enchanted village they go
On a river where the water starts its flow
I'd like to tell you where it is
But they said let no one know.

**37**

## Wonderful Cornwall

No one can visit Cornwall
Without a longing to return
For what the eyes have seen
The heart will always yearn.
The heavens quite often open
In May you'll take a chance
But if luck is with you
You'll win a summer in advance.
The byways on the south coast
Have long since been a favourite of mine
They're a gift for the avid walker
And come close to the divine.
If you have a love for hiking
You can walk your feet 'til sore
And tread elevated footpaths
Where warm winds caress the jagged shore.
Bathed in brilliant Cornish light
On giddy height where flowers blow
That gild the rugged coastline
Like multi coloured snow.
There are endless breaks along the route
Call at Fowey or romantic Looe
They have a touch of Enid Blyton
And of course Rebecca too.
There's the sweetest little harbours
They're best viewed from above
Where boys can dream of pirates
And little girls of love.
If you're feeling faint and hungry
Oh please do call into Looe

There are chips and Cornish pasties
But not much else to do.
You'll soon be on your travels
Along winding unnamed lanes
Seeking out the quaintest places
With their strangely foreign names.
Yes Cornwall is quite bewitching
Like no other place I know
And for a magic honeymoon
There's no better place to go.
The very names ring with excitement
They each have a certain call
Veryan, Penpoll, St Blazey, Golant, St Veeps
Lansollas, Mevagissey, Lerryn and Trefawl.
So whoever visits Cornwall
Let me tell you once again
They are never really free
From that ever whispering refrain.
For Port Eliot, Wheel Betsey, Lanhydrock calls
Come back, come back, back to me again

Soon back in their little prefab
Built by yanks in forty-four
Their happiness is ever swelling
They couldn't ask for more.
Living as one in a cameo divine
Both share a golden feeling
That their sun will always shine.
Each day a wave of unruffled joy
This the last time to be a little girl
And for him to be a carefree boy.
For they have a nagging feeling
Both keep shedding from their mind
This blissful little Eden
Will soon all be left behind.

**38**

## Star Of The Show

"It's a wonderful life just being a wife
Can't think why they call me trouble and strife
I wash, darn, iron and cook
With so many jobs, my head's like a book.
I organise, agonise, advise and console
I fret and worry when he's out on parole
I remove, improve, I'm interior design
He says in the house that everything's mine.
I impede or encourage, he doesn't complain
When it all goes wrong, he just takes the blame
I'm his critique, mentor, tutor and friend
I'm sure I send him half round the bend.
I plot, scheme and tell porkies too
He says you can have it, I only want you
I'm a temptress; vamp the star of the show
He says I'm a sensation and can't let me go!
I'm kissed, cuddled, massaged and persuaded
I'm pacified, satisfied, loved and invaded
I'm spoilt, pampered, my pleasures are rife
I'm fabulous happy just being a wife."

## 39

### In Golden Heaven

"It's been an eternity of time
Since sweet May to December
But contrary to what I'm told
It's been the best time I remember.
I simply left work in September
And don't look forward to returning
A strange thing I've discovered
It's the life I have been yearning.
I'm told that house is boring
Well that's a lot of rot
I've never been as happy
It's a life that's just my slot.
I'm never short of things to do
No silly old boss to please
No rush and tear and schedules
My life is one long breeze.
In October we stayed with friends
In their little farm in Devon
We just went walking through the leaves
It was our golden heaven.

"This constant kicking in my tummy
Why did I ever think it funny?
We call it Sagittarius rising
But now my body's past disguising.
My bosoms are lactating
And I'm sick and tired of waiting
Holy Aquarius my waters have just broken
And I can tell you it's no token.

Oh quick I must ring Albert at the park
Damn he's having another nap...
That's the third time, he just isn't picking up
Oh God, I'm in a massive panic
For I'm no maternity mechanic.
Ouch I've just had a whopping pain
I think I'll have a lie down
No, there's another one again!
My brain is like the rumba
And I've lost the midwife's number
And Hero won't be back 'til two
Oh rage for a guardian angel
What on earth am I to dooo!!"

Maternity was found in the end
With the help of a taxi
And the aid of June her most valued friend.
Now Selsey's lying down in comfort
But she isn't much enthralled
But the midwife's in attendance
And she's quite efficiently installed.

**40**

## Progressing Normally

"I suppose this is the real thing
And it's happening to me
How I wish it were all over
And I could have a cup of tea.
My mouth is dry, my hands are cold
And I'm just feeling half alive
And if I am to tell the truth
It's because I'm really terrified.
She says it's all progressing normally
Whatever that may be!
That midwife she's a dazz
With her Irish manner and effervescent chatter
But it's mostly to herself
And about things that hardly matter.

"Oh mother of Jesus I've had a trying day.
That poor girl this morning, her afterbirth came first
and the baby came out backwards. My God I
thought the poor things head was going to come off!"

# 41

## **Mother Nature**

"I've been lying here in agony
And it's nearly half past three
I'm not feeling very dignified
I will tell you things that be.
All private parts are on display
My crumpet's exposed to every stare
Ouch there's another awful pain
Thank God for gas and air.
I've been here since one thirty
And now it's well past four
The midwife says push harder
But I'm already in a tug of war.
And if these contractions don't decide to stop
I think I'll leave this bed
And if I find that Mother Nature
I'll go and blip her on the head."

"Oh will ya be pushing a wee bit harder now.
You're not lying down on the beach you know.
Talking about holidays, me daughter she's married
an Eye-talian. He thinks he's going to be an opera
singer. Gawd almighty he makes such a noise as to
wake the dead, says I'm blind to his talent. I wish I
could be deaf to it too. Mind you he's a hell of a
good looking fella. They live in Naples, she keeps
going on about a holiday, but knowing my luck
everything goes wrong when I'm around.
Vesuvius would erupt, and we'd all be showered with
hot cinders while laying in the sun, and that's for sure."

"Now come along you're just doing fine."
"One big push and he'll be mine."
"There now...you've got a fine baby boy
And born on the 7th too he'll be full of luck and joy."
"And how are you feeling my little darling?"
"Just wonderful all my troubles are over."
"Oh such nonsense I hear ya saying
Over indeed, you've just had a bit of fun
Just let me be telling you now
Your troubles have only just begun."

Hero had called before at nine
The nurse had said, "Both doing fine
Just go along and have a peep
But don't dare wake them from their sleep."
Five hours on the wards now full of gloom
Disturbed only by laughter from a distant room.

Now everyone is sleeping
There's not the slightest noise
There's only our new mother
In the light of an angle poise.
As ever she is beguiling
She's cameod in Rembrandt style
Her image has transfixed him
He doesn't move for quite a while.
She makes a pretty picture
But no Madonna ever in the richest oils
Could scarcely match the impact
Of her living breathing toils.
Her tumbling hair in disarray
Still glows damp with perspiration
As she looks down in wonder
At the eyes of her creation.

And as usual she's smiling
But it is with a mother's joy
As by her flowing breast
She feeds their baby boy.
Our Hero is quite overcome
So he leans across the bed
And kisses the new mother
Softly on her damp head.
Then in that witchy moment
And just for a fleeting instant
His eyes are filled with tears
Lost in new born baby's scent.
Where these tears have come from
It's quite impossible to tell
Perhaps some new emotion
Or from a deep paternal well.

Back at the park Hero's left to ponder
"Four days without her
Can my heart or my love grow any stronger?"

# 42

## **Thoughts**

"All my lonely hour
Are full of daytime dreams
Of you and I and other things
Pale moon does shine
Our soft arms entwine
You are home and you are mine."

Albert is buoyant at the news of a boy. Unusually
buoyant. "I'd like you to call im Sam. I always
wanted a little boy called Sam, yer, all my life
I av. Thass a fack!
Birf an deff are the most commonest
miracles on Erff, oh yerr. But outta the two of em
birf is the most wonderfullest. It being quite an easy
job you know to kiwll somebody, but another cup of
tea to make a newun ya might say.
An ow it awll come about
is towally inexplainable! Darwin say that it awl started
with
little worms, that got bigger and better as they grow up
like.
And it awl got done over miwions of years under the
sea,
then we come along. But I find that wery 'ard to
compwehend.
I find it better to blame it awl onta God, it much simpla
to understand that way, oh yer.
But 'ere just you remember, noo born
babies are savages wot need a lot of civilizing or they
wiwl be savage tiwl the end of their days and thass a
fack."

**43**

## Home And Free

"Oh it's good to get back home
My home is love to me
Here is everything I want
And what is more I'm free.
This ancient black and white TV
No, colour doesn't matter
The grandfather clock ticks by the wall
In my room of happy clutter.
There are always lots of books to read
And there are treasures dear to me
Strange things found on holidays
And my big picture of the sea.
And here's my cosy kitchen
With a dresser made of pine
Full up with hanging cups and jugs
And rows of cheerful plates that shine.
Our happy bright new bedroom
The Victorian bed is deep and snug
It doesn't need a fitted carpet
Just a wonderful Chinese rug.
There's not much here of value
That's very plain to see
But let me tell you now
It's as good as the whole world to me."

Mum puts Sammy in a wooden box
Placed on the kitchen table
So as to keep an eye on him
And do everything she's able.

Mum's got to leave by Christmas
But she can help out for a while
She makes Selsey take it easy
Then sorts the whole shoot out
In her inimitable style.

**44**

## My Happiness Swells

How quiet the house, it's Christmas Day
All rumbling traffic sounds faded away
In our bleak garden a robin comes to sing
Bravely awaiting the coming of Spring.
"Snowflakes are falling from Heaven above
My guardian angels are surely in love
Our wonderful boy is asleep in his cradle
Safely on top of the old kitchen table.
The lights round the windows sparkle and glow
And shine on the leaves of my cut mistletoe
The meat in the oven sizzles and bubbles
So far away, far away everyday troubles.
My Johnny's been working all day in the park
Soon he'll be home for it's almost dark
Candles are burning on hooks on the wall
Lighting the tinsel that hangs in the hall.
So my happiness swells for today and my boys
But sorrow for those who haven't my joys."

Things were hectic after mum had gone
And also a trifle scary
While rushing all about
And nursing her new fairy.
There's not much time to think
With so many things to do
All alone and late at night
With skills completely new.
And ever she is fretting
When he stirs there in his sleep

God has his little heart stopped
Or has it missed a beat?
So often she just marvels
At the fleeting smiles in his eyes
Brings to her strange feelings
A crescent moon in winter skies.
His clawing little hands
And his tiny little feet
She wonders will he ever grow up
Will he run, walk, laugh or speak?

Her nights are scattered memories
Her days are endless long
All sorts of things and jumbles
Just a never ending song.
Then life takes on a rhythm
Like breakers on the shore
But ever she is fighting work
There's always one job more.
Then as weeks turn into months
And all fears at last they fall away
One day she wakes up feeling fine
To a beautiful fresh spring day.
They're off down Drakefield Gardens
To the fish shop in Nunhead Lane
Beneath the nodding cherry blossom
And Sammy cooing in the pram
That sails ahead as light as air
Passers smile and nod admiringly
They make a pretty pair.

"Who wants a job I'll not go back
After my allotted time
If you want to get up early

You certainly can have mine.
Who wants to load up biscuits?
Or an endless conveyor line
Or work the dread computer
You take my job, that's fine.
Who wants to drive in traffic jams?
To get to work on time
Call that your independence
You certainly can have mine.
Who wants to give away their children?
For what seems an endless age of time?
To give another girl a job, pooie
Well she'll not be getting mine
For I adore my little Sammy
And I want him all the time
My life is to make ends meet
Who wants a job? Take mine!"

At the park Hero is limping. "You tewl me you
caught your ankle on the pwam in the awl,
that is wery serious. There was a famous bloke
oo ad a load of gewls but never wed none of em
awl because e lived in total tewor of a pwam in the
awl. There is a undwed places that she could putit
but in the awl. But it's a signal to the ole wewld that
she as cweated a new uman bein and avin a wery ard
time. Wewll don't you believe it, she is avin the time
of her life and it don't never get betta, oh yer. And
summink ewlse, you could git gangoring in that leg
and be serwiously decommissioned or die, oh yer!"

"My peaceful life has changed
To one of harmonious intrusion
Sweeter than a working girl's

With her turbulent confusion.
The chaos screams and clatter
It doesn't seem to matter anymore
The never ending nappies
And all that baby clutter on the floor.
It's a time you have to go through
But there are joys along the way
He's an engaging little fellow
I'll not miss a single day.
You may think they're all the same
But there's always something new
Yesterday he caught his finger in the door
Today he lost his little shoe.
Last week he turned 18 months
And he hasn't said a word
Well maybe he could have
But nothing I have heard.
Now there's that little goldfinch
Who sits on our window sill."
Sammy shouted, "Look! Look!"
"That really was a thrill."
It's funny how things change
In top gear for that first year
Now the third year has arrived
Life's slipped down to second gear.
Hero's home to lunch most days
"My day's made up of little things
Do you know I even get excited
When we're going to the swings
And so my little life keeps turning
I'm happy as can be
There are lots of things to teach him
But he often teaches me.
Now that he is walking and talking

We call it foot and mouth disease
He asks me a thousand questions
I'll do anything to please.
All week I have been wondering
How does the air get in the bubble?
Little questions like that
Yes, they give me a bit of trouble.
He turned the telly upside down
And kicked it all about
And when I asked him why he'd done it
'To let the man fall out.'
All the things he does aren't funny
And they often make me shout
But the day he kicked the telly
Made me fall about.
Well now I must be going
I've got a load of things to do
I'll have to make a picnic now
I'm taking Sammy to the zoo.
We're off to Crystal Palace
So we can see the monsters too
There's a boating lake as well
So there are all sorts of things to do."

"Last year he sent a Christmas card
I'll keep it 'til my dying day
He said he really liked the words
About the squirrel in its dray
And this is how it goes...

"In the shed the cows are lowing
Bitter winds have stopped their blowing
In the woods the barn owl calls
Uncaring of the snow that falls.

The wise squirrel slumbers in its dray
Tomorrow will be Christmas Day."

He got June across the way to write
His little Christmas greetings
She said the words were his
They're so sweet they take some beating.
"Dear mum and dad
Hope Father Christmas gives you all the things you
want."

"He loves the squirrels in the garden
And mad on birds of prey
He rushes out to see them
But can't think why they run away.
But it's my eternal pleasure
Just to sit and watch him play
And if I were born again
I wouldn't want it any other way."

Sweets June's come round again
And the bower's looking smart
Five years it has been growing
From its very shaky start.

**45**

## SONNET: For The Rose

Fair rose my love, rich joy you bring to England's
gardens
Standing proud in your Tudor privilege
Born of the hedgerows, but now in royal garlands.
Please grant me licence to flatter
For indeed you are queen among the many
Who could dare stand in for love's red rose?
Your realm be safe, with few rivals, if any.
How I puzzle the mystery of your design
To draw from the bitter depths such honeyed scent
And sweet the rainbow hues, yet androgynous you are
Clothed in savage barbs that claw and rent.
Come June, it's yours to crown the summer's bounty
No other blossom has such glory or talent for
diversities
But ever you are undaunted by winter's cruel
adversities.

"It's a great change to be a father
And now that Sammy's four
He's a splendid little fellow
And quite easy to adore.
I used to think I'd like a girl
But now I've got Sam I want no other
He's full of joyful mischief
And always smiling like his mother.

Last year I took my driving test
It's great I'm qualified

They let me use the park van
So often I'm free to drive.
Fryer he's away plant hunting
Albert's gone to convalescence
So I'm in charge and free
Well that's how it feels in essence.
Lunchtime I'll get Sammy
Bring him back here for a run
It's nice to have him here
We always have a lot of fun.
When I go to fetch him
In my dinner hour
Both will be there waiting
Beneath our scented bower.
Ever pleased to see me
With eyes there shining bright
As always they'll be smiling
With undisguised delight"

On his arrival later
There's no one by the bower
But Sammy tells his father
"Mummy's washing in the shower."
She soon comes out smiling
Just a towel around her waist
"I want to come along with you
That's if you're in no haste.
There's a jumble sale at Peckham
I must have a root around
Do you remember last month?
The lovely things I found."

That sounds a pretty reason
But the story isn't really true

It's because there's nothing here on earth
That can get between those two.
Soon they drive off all smiles
As if going to the moon
With Sammy springing on her knee
She smiles and sings a little tune.

# 46

## <u>Smiles</u>

The smile that slides across the room
Warms your heart with joy and ease
A welcome in a stilted place
Like a perfumed April breeze.
That smile that breaks the ice
And can do considerably more
If turned into a smirk
Could even start a war.
A smile so often fleeting
And never can be heard
But sends an instant message
More explicit than a word.
Of all the little come ons
That can push you on a mile
What use a dancing bosom?
Without a knowing smile.
A smile is never purchased
Though sometimes put on order
It's been seen to open doors
And can ease you over a border.
An untimely one can infuriate
And can easy burst your bubble
Beware that dread careless one
That causes so much trouble.
Smiles cannot be stolen
Safe deep down in the hold
Costs nothing to the giver
To the receiver can be gold.
A smile can speak a tragedy

That one that masks a sorrow
The awful goodbye smile
That says there can be no tomorrow.

"Hope you don't mind me tagging on
I've got to rush to catch that jumble
I think I bought the clouds
Did you hear that thunder rumble?"
"Well Sel, whenever I have you near
The sunshine's already here.
If the day is dull it's no matter
We've no need for the clouds to scatter.
All we need is you and me
And Sammy, that's family.
When we're all together
Who cares about the weather?
You and Sammy's pitter-patter
Clouds, it just doesn't matter."

# 47

## The Joys Of Poverty

Selsey's at the church hall
She's way back in the queue
There's the usual motley crowd
They don't make a pleasant view.

The man with fingers missing
He lost them in Hitler's war
Insists on chatting Selsey up
Oh please don't do it anymore!

One couple wearing sixties flares
His chick a pink Madonna bra
Has no one ever told them?
Just how ridiculous they are.

The same old group of regulars
Packed tightly round the door
I'm told they're all one family
Don't give birth to anymore!

The tall chap halfway down
Books are his only passion
With his stark Reithian demeanour
And clothes way out of fashion.

There's three or four Neanderthals
Hardly in the human race
If you tried to find their relatives
They could be very difficult to trace.

Of the several unkempt ladies
Of indeterminate age
Most of who have children
That keeps them in a sort of rage.

They're scattered up and down the queue
From the front to back
And they are largely responsible
For the endless noisy track.

"Wayne, I see you do that Wayne
Dean you stop that you little bleeder
John put 'er daan! Daan I said!!
You aint gettin' no more sweets I'm tellin' ya."

All this crush and maybe more
Is what you'll be obliged to stand
Once you have become addicted
To the dread cult of second hand.

Soon the fight, the scramble's over
Like the extraction of a tooth
But of course she really loves it all
And that's the golden truth.

She's sitting in the back room
With buttered scones and tea
Sorting gleefully through her finds
Those simple joys of poverty.

Sam is with his father clearing up the Rye

It's an unpopular filthy job that really is a pain
With all that tacky litter blown from Rye Lane .

But Sammy being innocent and just a little boy
This irksome little number seems to fill him up with
joy.
He holds a handy-grabber much longer than he's high
And makes a speedy dash at everything that he can spy.
Dad just walks along behind with a great big plastic bag
And it's wonderful how quickly it's filled and starts to
sag.
Soon there are four bags full and it seems the job is
done
So Sammy runs behind the mower that's his idea of fun.
Soon covered all over with grass he's smelling pretty
strong
And all the time's he's yelling this funny little song.

"I'm a little green man that's what I am
And everybody knows my name is Sam
All the grass is mowed away
So no more daisy chains today
When the clouds fall down and rain
Well, I'll kick them up again
I'll run and run and run away
All on a hot and humm...ers day – Hooray!"

**48**

## Love Of Sam

"Why is your heart so big, so full of joy?
When you are such a tiny boy
Your smile seems bigger than your face
Yet sits in such a little space.
Why is my love for you so tall?
When you are so very small
I love to touch your golden hair
Even though there's not much there.
I often wonder how you're so brave
When not armed with stick or stave
Is there nothing in your mind
That makes you scared or fall behind?"
"Yes dad, clouds that rush across the sky
How do they get up there so high?"
"Oh Sam, I just can't explain
That's water so it should be down the drain."
"But dad, they may fall down with lots of rain
Then you can kick them up again."
"So Sammy boy don't be afraid
When clouds cast down their gloomy shade
Or build marble castles up on high
Or hang coloured curtains in the sky.
So if clouds fall down and rain
Just laugh and kick them up again
Oh Sammy even though you are so small
You are my triumph and my all.
And even when the skies are dark
There's always sunshine in your heart."

They're all back in the shed
It's time for tea and cakes
At weekends there's not many there
So they're feeling pretty free.
She got a brooch at the jumble
That glitters and looks old
It's also very beautiful
She thinks it may be gold...it isn't.

Albert's back from convalescence, it's Monday
And the weather's such a pain
All weekend it's been rodding down
With endless, endless rain.
"'Ere Johnny, if you git a lull in the wain
git Sid to take you on the twactor and make
sure all them dwains is gittin away or we'll get
all them bweeding dog walkers rand 'ere
compwainin oh yer! There's puddawls as big as
miwllponds all over, and thass a fack, oh yer!"

It's late afternoon, Albert is gazing out of the
window at the sheets of rain. It's been falling
all day, mind wetting, foot rotting and all but
never ending. Peter the propagator plods about
uncaring of the water in his great green wellingtons.
The yard and the glasshouses are already an inch deep
in water. Peter thinks it's fine, just fine. Albert pulls a
pile of tissues from his pocket and wipes his great
gooseberry nose. "Bweeding August, oh yer!" He then
sits down to read his latest book, A Brief History Of
Time.
After an hour of ceaseless reading only broken by the
occasional grunt or sigh, he suddenly jumps up and
looks

out at the pouring rain. He then holds his head between his big hands as if to squeeze a thought from his brains. "A 'orrible fought 'as just come acwoss my mind, that bweeding fair is coming at the end of the week, that is going to be twouble, big twouble, oh yer!"

**49**

## <u>Elephants</u>

The fair comes to Peckham only once a year
You can bet that it will rain
Of that you have no fear
The tents leave big green circles
That takes months to disappear.
A circus is really much more fun
Last time they came with elephants
And left a ton or more of dung
They kindly dropped it in a tent
Lovely for the garden
And of course that's where it went.

On Wednesday Albert and Hero are on the Rye
It's raining! "Oh it don't look good a awl, not a awl.
Jus' look at them puddawls, you wouldn't dare
step in em for fear of your bweeding life, oh yer!"
Albert turns to make for the hut
"It's 'ard to compwe-end that the 'ole place wyll be
a bweeding mad'ouse in juss a foo days, an utter
mad'ouse oh yer!"

Oh yes, indeed like last year.

**50**

## Fair On The Rye

Hoards of young yobs will swarm up from Rye Lane
From the little side roads and alleys
That lay behind the shops
More still from the council estates.
The no-go places of Queens Road
They'll come yelping and bellowing
Barking like seals in their new found manhood
Bringing with them their girls
Scantily dressed, squawking, hooting and giggling.
Their libido bubbling over with confidence
All shapes, weights and sizes
The coarse and ugly the cheap and gaudy
The good lookers flashing their bodies off
With an intent that would put a male in prison.
Janice Dally six foot in her birthday suit
Savagely peroxided hair touching her bottom
She's repellent and attractive in one
Common as dirt desirable as gold
Braless and without stockings
Smoking provocative and cocky.
Those high heels, those legs, wow
She should have a license for them
She may get a shag on the Rye if she's lucky
If she's unlucky!
Small groups of twelve year olds
Sweet bewildered, smiling and unnoticed
Just a chocolate bar and makeup in their purse
Mum said "Don't go to the fair, it's rough,"
She could have saved her breath

Big, loud, frightening girls, rough and rude
They're overweight they're overfed.
Take Pauline Boughfront
Her McGill arse could block a doorway
And a bosom to match of course
She smiles at any boy she fancies
With her joyous pork pie face
White as flour and as plump as a baby's bottom.
She rushes off to the wall of death terrors
Where nobody ever dies
Then the hurdy-gurdy, helter skelter thrills
To spread her fleshy thighs on precarious seats
To be hurtled bumped tossed and shaken
Then lifted and suddenly dropped
Hugging herself or anybody nearby.
Gulping with terror and screaming in unison
Again to be flung, jarred and spun like a top
And then vomited into space.
Drowned in her adrenalin
Numbed by the noise of the generators
Deafened by pulsating music
Blinded by a million watts of lights
In a Valhalla of shrieking joy
Later to be decanted into the night.
Penniless, shaking and dazed
It all ends in tears as always
She's left her purse in the tunnel of love
But the boys are spoiling for a fight.
Rival gangs scowl at each other
Plumbers' mates, builders, labourers, barrow boys and
drivers
Everyone knows everyone
Broad shouldered big fisted thugs
Could knock you out or break your jaw with one punch

Or kick you to death, it's been done!
They've just come tanked up
Straight from the Kings Arms
Keep away, don't even look at them
They could cost you your front teeth.
Gangs of surly creeps looking for easy money
Temporarily out of prison permanently out of work
Ignorant clueless and lazy
The heaviest things they've ever pushed are drugs.
Someone's going to be mugged
Somebody's going to be beaten up
There'll be a big fight, there always is
The iron men and gyppos that run the place
Oblivious to fear and say nothing
But keep a hammer or iron bar handy
And keep a close eye on their cash.
There's hardly a rozzer in sight
They're lurking round The Gardens
Packed like sardines in their unlit vans
Smoking and bemoaning their lot
Smug in their deep blue authority
Friendly but insidious, keep away!
Don't even look at them
They could cost you money
They're waiting for the call that always comes
Back up! There's been another friendly stabbing.

It's three o'clock on Thursday and rain is still falling
In the fuggy humid hut Albert suddenly gets up
And throws the book he's been reading
Into the rubbish bin.
"Brief 'istory of time seems like an eternity to me
I've been reading it...'ees got an extweemly wirulent
imagination, that bloke 'oos wrote it. I'm not 'arf an

atom wiser than when I star'id, oh yer!"
He goes to the window and stares for a long while
at the now flooded yard. He then turns to Hero.
"Listen 'ere Johnny, I've gotta tewl yew sumfing
Lookin out of that window put me in mind of when
I was a pwisoner of war. I was always lookin outta
my cewll window. All ya could see was a little bitta
land, what nobody used and didn't never see no-one.
Jus' a foo bushes like, and twees and fings. But in the
spwing it awl come up wiv weeds and wiawld flowers
like. Then come wintta time, it awl come dan to nuffin.
Up and dan, up and dan every year, then one year a
littawl bird come dan and buiwld a nest outside my
winda and then pu'eggs init like, and when the eggs
'atched and the littawl birds come out the muvva bird
fly
back an' forward wiv littawl bits of food like. It keep
coming back and forward, to and fwo, awl day long.
Once
I keep count of it like, and it come by more than fwee
'undred times before dark. As time went by it calmed
my bwain dan, an' I gotta finkin that littawl bird doin
all
that work and me, I'm ere jus doin nuffin. So I made a
pwomise to myself, that if I ever get out, I'd learn all
abou'flowers and twees and birds and fings, oh yer! An'
then I did and that's what I dun. I get myself a littawl
house and 'av a garden wiv flowers and twees so birds
come to my garden everyday, so I 'av got myself
wisdom wot is wery 'ard to find these days. Not like
that book that don't meannuffin to nobody, but could
cause gweat bewilderment to the 'uman mind, oh yer
an thass a bweeding fack."

**51**

## The Schedule

In the park beneath the trees
Where flowers nod there in the breeze
To the common eye looks sweet and bright
But alas, all things are not right.
Regimented beds may look all at ease
But to some they do displease
Those awful begonias, row on row
Not the sort of thing I'd like to show.
Venomous Salvias looking like a flood
Filling up the centre like a river of blood
Oh how people love them there in every seaside town
Go to Eastbourne, their beds are quite renowned.
Now there's a secret that is horrible
It's all done to a strict schedule
All things in the beds have their allotted day
Wallflowers go for the chop some sunny day in May.
Rooted out and piled up as if they're mown hay
But that isn't where they'll stay
Old ladies come and help themselves. Incredible
You see they know the schedule
And I'm told by these old dears
They double their size and soldier on for years.
So Salvias, Marigolds and Begonias row on row
To jog along with Dahlias for the summer show
Dahlias will happily flower 'til first frost
But all too soon their chances are completely lost.
On the day and without warning
With no respect for global warming
Quite suddenly they're gone, it's incredible

The old ladies come because they know the schedule.
And pop a few tubers in their bin
Then scrounge a few bulbs that should be going in
Soon after spring's first glory's past
Wind, frost that first show never lasts.
No sign of those old ladies, I feel a trifle lost
Maybe they all went with that first heavy frost
Perhaps the affluent society or dementia, incredible
They may have just forgotten the schedule
So to the beat of the eternal drum
Busy Lizzy, Salvias, Fucias and Begonias, here we come!
But, there is one thing that's incredible
And can really upset the schedule
It's that eternal rain, rain, rain
And that's what it's doing now, oh pain!


The fair arrived yesterday and the strong men weren't
happy at what they saw. Worse was to come. In the
hour
of darkness the Victorian brick culvert that carries the
old
river Peck couldn't take the strain. It broke, flooding
the
Rye with dubious water, deep enough to get into the
already sinking caravans. The men are furious, their
women are disgusted, they've had enough and want no
more of Peckham Rye. They're not paying, they're not
staying so the usual silent gypsies and strong men are
out
shouting and cursing, drenched and unhappy,
cigarettes
clenched in their bony fists. But things are looking up.
Their big vintage Scammal tugger is making light work
of

a bad thing. What a tool. All radiator, wheels and
chassis.
Its mighty engine has enough torque to drag the devil
out
of hell. Since eight o'clock she's been roaring and
juddering belching fire like a dinosaur on heat. By ten
she's pulled all of the heavy equipment and caravans
from
the mud. They're off. They have another site to set up in
Ramsgate. Albert surveys the damage that looks pretty
muchlike Passchendaele. "An' bwoody good widdence
to 'em, oh yer! Now Johnny, let's nip acwoss the woad
to the cafe and 'av a nice cuppa tea and a bacon woll
and I wiwl pay, oh yer!!"

After the excitement of the flood
The broken culvert and endless mud
Repairing that was a lot of fun
But then we got the sun, sun, sun
Two months it shone without falter
Scorching our sunbathers altar.

**52**

## Weather Tether

Oh forever our eternal changing weather
What would we do without the weather?
For most our small talk there we tether
Turned out nice in the end
You don't have to tell me
I've lugged this mackintosh around all day
How was the cricket boy?
All a flaming washout wasn't it?
Couldn't see the ball for rain
Better check your anti-freeze
It's going down below zero tonight
Already is, I can't wait for this global warming thing
Did you hear that wind last night?
Hear it? Blew my fence down, didn't it!
Wind, it's the house owner's enemy
What would we do without the weather
For most our small talk there we tether.

# 53

## Autumn

Autumn's here the year is turning
And for the past our heart's be yearning
Spooky mists lurk on the Rye
Seen by early risers passing by.
Sad days of ever shorter length
As the sun is losing strength
It may well be growing old
But outshines the fading Marigold.
The office blocks a shade too hot
For the sun shines at a lower slot
The city workforce sit and laze
Not long back from distant holidays.
Crave summer's bounty that last drop
Before wet and windy calls a stop
But blue skies warm winds still prevail
And tug gently at the surfer's sail.
In the cornfields sparrows gleaning
The fatted kestrel on its spire preening
That tête a tête ends far too soon
In gorgeous turquoise afternoon.
Screeching swifts have long since gone
To leave us with the blackbird song
Shipleys mill turns on its spindle
By the woods of swirling brindle.
Old Betty's homebrew clears to gold
And her garden robin's getting bold
Cocks its head and gets the worms
As the earth she digs and turns.
Twilight lovers kiss and swoon

Gilded by the hunter's moon
Its luminous disc sits by the hill
To add romance and honey to their thrill.
The silent owl stares from the bough
And George still tinkers with the plough
With darkness comes October's chill
Oak logs burn chestnuts roasting on the grill.
In the East, Orion comes in sight
Soon to dominate the sky at night.

Oh how sweetly the summer turned to fall
That we were scarcely aware of it all
Young girls still wear summer fare
That sun, we seem to have an extra share.
Old folks said, it must be some kind of trick
I can't remember a summer like it
So that avid Fryer had a bright idea
To celebrate the seasons end of year.
For further education, not a lark
A wonderful coach trip to Sheffield Park
There the autumn colours to admire
With the hope the staff it will inspire.

It could have been a wonderful day
Then things went seriously astray
Some said it fate, others said it very odd
Albert of course said, "It were act of God."
It's always nice to get out of town
Then a classic garden by Capability Brown
The crowded cafe made you want to hide
The beauty of the garden couldn't be denied.
So the driver and Fryer had a little chat
Off to Devils Dyke and that was that
The elder members of the staff, oh dear

They lusted after hot lunch and beer.
Oh the weather was too good to be true
Para gliders hanging in a halcyon sky of blue
Selsey had some food and a blanket too
So they had a picnic somewhere out of view.

As soon as Selsey had cleared away Hero shook the blanket, spread it on the grass then lays down on it. For a moment, gazes into the deep azure of the afternoon sky, then closes his eyes, feels a light playing breeze and hears drifting summer sounds.

Selsey clothed in a simple cotton dress sits with her back to the sun absorbing the pressing warmth. Motionless and dreaming. She looks out over the rich green and gold patchwork of the Sussex Weald and on into the blue haze of the North Downs. She fancies she can see Box Hill, but she's not sure. In her mind's eye she sees London hidden beyond then dreams of her little prefab. "Isn't life wonderful" she murmurs to herself. She imagines June across the way, "She'll be sitting on her patio sunning herself no doubt. Poor June, she told me she hadn't had a climax for ages and even when she does they're like crumpled yellow pages. Oh God, mine are still purple and gold. I'm so lucky. Poor June."

While they'd been eating, Sammy had noticed that birds had been flying into nearby bushes. He had wondered why so many had come to such a small amount of shade. Perhaps it was the shelter they were after, but from what? Now he's going to investigate, but something else has caught his eye. The silvery sky to the south has turned a dull blue, then to grey and even darker.

His little face drains with instinctive apprehension. Hero in
his half sleep hears Sammy's plaintive cry. "Daadee, daadee, clouds are coming."
"Well kick them back again."
But Sammy continues, "Mummy, mummy." But Selsey is lost in dreaming and is unhearing. A sudden chill draught makes her shiver and lifts a lock of her golden russet hair and flicks it forward over her shoulder. Looking up, she can't make out why all the para gliders are coming down towards her, in big swooping loops.
Meanwhile, the draught has turned into an uncomfortable icy wind that tears at her flimsy dress. Suddenly the bright sunlight vanishes. At the same moment Sammy lets out a long shriek of terror. Selsey jumps up and runs towards him only to be met by a painful wall of hailstone, swirling and bouncing with intense fury. Sammy's swept up and in an instant they're all sheltering under the bushes, covered with the blanket as best they can.
The sky continues to darken only to be lit up like a supernova by a cruel fork of lightning. Then an instant boom of thunder that shakes the chalk beneath them. The two para gliders straggling behind are struck and plummet in flames, down down to the bottom of the dyke. Visibility becomes limited, just the sound of people shouting and the screams of a woman in the eerie darkness. Within minutes it's all over. Leaving a scene of dazed people and a vista of blinding incandescence
as the sun regains its hold.

A big red sun is sinking down
Gilding the traffic leaving town

144

They're in the coach and gently rocking
In Hero's mind that scene so shocking.
Could those men still be alive or dead?
The thought just won't leave his head
The coach jogs on through Norwood
Selsey's mind just won't move forward.
Sammy starts school in New Year
And that time comes dreadful near
It won't seem right without him around
His noise is such a pleasing sound.
Those school outfits cost a few bob
"I suppose… I'll have to find a job."
And as the coach slows to a stop
"Look Johnny outside that shop."
A bill board, "FREAK STORM KILLS TWO"
Well I guess I always knew.

**54**

## Talking Gobbley

Selsey's standing at the door
With poor June across the way
She's come over for a chin wag
And has nothing definite to say.
The chatter goes from whispers
To words of massive magnitude
Are they sharing secrets
Or saying something very rude?
There's a large amount of laughter
And lots of No's and Yeah
But to Sam it's all a gobbley
It's just a waste of air.
"Aw, they were really gorgeous
I should've bought those shoes
But there's a closing down at Ballworth
And a giant sale at S and Q's."
"Mum, please go to the shops tomorrow
I need a big sail for my boat."
"Oh bless him he's such a little dear
But looks like he needs a coat."
Sammy's had his ear cocked
But can't make much sense of what they say
He's feeling rather chilly
June please come in or go away.
"I think I'll go tomorrow
Peeks have got a half price slash
I bet it's just like last year
Just a load of tatty trash.
Oh if my hubby could only see my card

But he knows that I can't stop
And with me he's never hard."
"Mum, mum let's go to the shop."
Then Sammy interrupts again
"They might have a half price slash
I wouldn't have to wait for birthday
Or that horrid Christmas rush."
The postman joins them by the bower
"Hello, what are you doing son?"
"I'm starting school soon
It's going to be a lot of fun."
"I bet you'd like to take your mum with you."
"Oh no, she knows everything"
June explodes with laughter
Then stoops down and kisses him
She adores our little Sammy
"How I wished that he was mine."
Pressing money in his hand, "Bye Sam,"
She does that every time
That June's as sweet as sugar
And as peaceful as a dove
She's ever on an even keel
The sort of girl that you could love.

Next day Hero's in the top nursery
And that's where Hero likes to stay
If he knew what hell was coming
He'd pray or simply run away.
No one likes to work here
It's fenced in and tucked away
Just beyond the arboretum
But always makes a peaceful day.
There's compost heaps to turn
And ever present weeds a pig

It's the storehouse of the park
So there's endless beds to dig.
Here you could find a stunted tree
So ask if you can take it
And if you have the time and skill
You could make a bonsai of it.
Albert was in an awful grump
When Hero came to start his day
And after the proverbial monologue
He felt quite pleased to get away.
"This morning I was wery annoyed at what
I av just 'eard. The carnciwl 'av jus given Mr
Fwyer a first class award, an award for the
Dahlia display in the owd English garden.Wewl
'e aint dun nuffing! We 'ave planted 'em. We 'ave
dug big 'oles and we ave fiwlled 'em up wiv
wotted compost, an' we 'ave staked 'em up and
'e go n get the award! All 'e done was to tewl us
where ta put the toobers, as if we don't
bweeding know, oh yer. People in this wewld that
get titles an' wear medawls are always the ones
oo don't never deserve 'em oh yer. Take them
admiwals and genewals that ang abaut in white
awl, oo don't never get kiwlled an av so many
medawls , that if they put em all on at once they
would get top evvy and fawl dan the bweeding
stairs, oh yer. And as for Mr Fwyer getting that award
I will tewll you ow e dunnit. 'ee give that lady
Mayoress one of 'is Californian camillias, and what
is worser e gave er a load of is Scottish charm and
that is a bweeding fack!"

Two beds dug and smelling sweet
It's just eleven o'clock

But Albert appears calling, running
And that's something of a shock.
He's a man who never runs
But the news he brings is stunning
It puts him in a dreadful state
Gasping, puffing as he's running.
"'Er acwoss the woad, June 'as jus wung and there's
bin a 'owwible accident. Your wife is in awspital,
you betta take the van and get over there quick.
It sounds wery, wery sewious indeed."

An agitated Hero arrives at the hospital
His mind is racing and he's doubly confused
He can't seem to find a person
Who can furnish him any news.
Everyone looks fraught with worry
And they're all rushing to and fro
They will not give him eye contact
But they all know where to go.
At last he's found some authority
And is standing by the desk
His poor mind still racing madly
And his comprehension in a mess.

# 55

## My Head's In A Bottle

"Mr Smith?"
"Yes."
"Is Mrs Smith your spouse?"
"No she's my wife."
"Her date of birth please."
"Er… she's a Libra."
"Oh, what day in October?"
"I can't remember."
"Would you like a cup of tea, sir?"
"No I don't think I should."
"Why?"
"I've had one this morning."
"Do you cohabitate?"
"What do you mean?"
"Do you live together?"
"Oh yes, there's no other place."
"What is your code?"
"Code number, I haven't got one."
"Oh post code, sir."
"Is she a British subject?"
"No, she's not subject to anything."
"Where was she born?"
"Clapham I think."
"Full name of next of kin please."
"Who's that?
"Er…it's me I suppose
"That's John Hero Smith."
"And your date of birth?"
"I…was…I can't think."

"Now go along to A&E."
"What's that?"
"Accident area, sir."
"That sounds dangerous."
"No it's quite safe
"Just follow the red line
"Then find Mary Hubbards ward.
"Ask for Dr Burrows.
"Oh thank you very much.
"Er...Dr Tunnel?"
"No, Burrows, Dr Burrows."
After many dead ends the ward was found
"Could I speak to Dr Warren?"
"There's no doctor here of that name, sir."
"Er... no... I mean Dr Warren or Burrows."
"Oh yes that's me."
"I'm enquiring about Mrs Selsey Smith my wife."
"Ah yes, Mrs Smith, follow me."
Hero is led into a small room
His heart is pounding and feels slightly dizzy
She's just been given the once over.
"We thought she may have broken her back
But I'm pleased to tell you she's A1, not a scratch."
He walks to Selsey who's lying on a small iron bed
She looks more like Hollywood's Sleeping Beauty
And much less like an accident and emergency
The doctor lifts her arm up and checks her pulse
Then drops it, "You see there's no response at all
We think she's in some kind of traumatic shock
It could last for hours, maybe days or even longer
And even when she does eventually pull through
There could be serious long term effects."
"Where is Sammy? Who's looking after him?"

"Oh the little fellow was air lifted to Great Ormond
Street
I'm afraid he was rather poorly I believe
But at the moment that's all I can tell you."
Hero's by her bed. He takes a long look at Selsey
The sort of look you give your first born
Not sure whether touching is in order
He brings his lips down to her ear
So close as to be a kiss, and whispers
"Don't fade honey bunch, I love you
But I must leave you, I've got to find Sam."
At the sound of his name her body stiffens
And just for a moment her eyes flick open
Then she sinks down again to an impenetrable sleep.

Outside it's raining and a ticket on the van
"Oh God, my life is such a pain
If I could find that parking warden
It would be a pleasure to annihilate his brain!!"

At the hut Albert expresses it with his usual rude
eloquence. "We live in a wewld of infinite wonder
and complex Darwinian beauty wot 'as been sent
from God. All alone in the universe, a fing that 'as
never bin the likes of for biwions of year, or peraps
never again! An wot av we got ended up wiv,
tewwowists, parking tickets an speed bumps. They
awl want flattening out, oh yer. Ever since the
womans come 'ere and invented woads, we 'av bin
twying to smoov em out, and now we 'av dunnit
along come some idiot block 'ed an put wery big bumps
wot nobody don't want, wight in the middowl of the
woad an er... oh yer." He comes to a slow halt realising
he's on sensitive ground, but he needn't have worried.

Hero isn't listening, he's got the A-Z and is finding a bus
route to Great Ormond Street hospital.

It is with foreboding and trepidation
He finally arrives at his destination
But bright smiling nurses welcome him
And a friendly doctor fills him in.

June had come along with Sammy
So upset, soon sent home by taxi
It seems that with her very eyes
She had witnessed poor Sammy's demise.
And she fainted twice while waiting
Then needed calming and sedating
Now Hero gets his first scare
Through the doors marked Intensive Care.

## 56

### Be My Hero Born

"Hello, I'm Sam's surgeon"
"Surgeon? What surgeon for God's sake?
I know that...he is...poorly
Just tell me there's been some mistake."

"There's been massive cranial haemorrhage
I'm afraid there's very little hope
You must prepare yourself for the worst."
The words stick in his throat.

The words come like a knockout punch
But that is all they can say to you
When they've tried everything
And there's no more they can do.

Hero's in a trance like shock
Hears rushing in his head like a speeding train
The walls begin to rock and sway
A gasping in his chest that's bordering on pain.

The room seems filled with water
And he can no longer stand
His vision is reeling his head is sinking
Down into the darkness of his hand.

One arm outstretched he's falling, falling
Soon down upon one knee
Hears sounds of howls and sobbing
Scarcely knowing that it's he.

Our broken Hero kneels there weeping
Just balanced as best he's able
Feels a hand rest on his shoulder
The loving hand that rocked the cradle.

Through his pain he feels her calling
"Johnny though your heart be torn
Stand up now and face your turmoil
Now you must be my Hero born."

He stands up rather unsteadily
That is with the aid of a nurse
He goes to look at Sammy
That makes him feel much worse.

And in that dread moment knows
That the future does look black
His life will change forever
And he never can go back.

When people are in shock
Some laugh, while others cry
But there's another group
That fall asleep or maybe die.

He sits on a chair beside Sam
Holds his sweet clammy little hand
And in an instant he's asleep
A dreadful shallow fitful sleep.

Full of dark and sinister shapes
Dull houses with broken windows
Hateful, morbid and unendingly sad
Matched only by the ghastly reality of waking.

It's five thirty in the morning
A nurse holds a cup of steaming tea
I'm going off duty take this
He gazes into the little whirlpool of tea.
It isn't the best cup of tea in the world
He thinks it looks a bit wishy washy
She's so busy but she's taken time
Thank you, thank you nurse.
Suddenly he's overcome with gratitude
Tears run down his face and fall to the floor
Soon the nurse is gone
And then Hero to face his day.

In the rush hour turmoil he feels zombie like
Things have changed, his mind is numb
He feels as if he's in a bottle
And isolated from the world outside
That rushes by at hectic speed.
Inside the bottle time is a step behind
Worse still someone's put the cork in
Sounds seem to come from a great distance
Aren't clear and have no vital meaning.

He arrives at Dulwich hospital
Then finds Selsey as if on auto pilot
Sits by her bed and talks.
Suddenly it's two thirty
He leaves and hasn't said goodbye
At the park the girls question him
Enquiries clog his delirious brain
Like soggy muffins unable to be digested
Most questions just go unanswered
They cook a meal for him in the hut
But he can't quite understand why.

Later he calls to see June
She sobs and is mostly incoherent
What is sad and most painful
She blames herself for everything.
"If I hadn't been there talking
All this would have never happened."
Her husband tells the whole story
"The car hit a keep left island
A safety island so high the car bounced
Mounted the pavement and er... hit Sam."
"Oh I'm so sorry about Sam"
June says it over and over again.

Back in the sad desolation of his home
The full horror of things become apparent
It seeps into his brain, then his bones
But he's too numb to feel the full impact.
Still fully clothed he lays on the bed
Soon to enter that same dreadful sleep
And that same painful shock of awakening
It's Wednesday, it will be the same.
A mirror of all the allotted days of Pathos
Pitiful little Sam in the morning
The unshakeable dreaming Selsey thereafter.
As the desolate days drag forlornly by
Hero begins to feel like Albert's bird
To and fro, back and forth in his prison
His torpor is replaced by anger
Anger grows into fear and rage
And oh how he rages about Sammy's smashed face
And all the other joyless broken children
Then fury, fury for himself, "Why me?!"
This lonely and unseen cross and evil karma
The only sane thing is the ever pleasant nurses.

# 57

## A Scream In My Head

"My happy little world has split in two
And I'm sure I'm on the rotten half
Oh how I long to get back
But it's clear to see there is no path.
I'm feel I'm hanging on a hook
With a starless sky above
Take me down, take me down
Please go on give me a shove.

"Let the devil have my soul
I need a happy drug to rush through my veins
And I'm craving for a spirit
That will permeate my brains.
I have a raging anger
And a fear that will not wane
Also a constant terror of this thing
That may shake my kaleidoscope of pain.

"I want to weep I want to sleep
I want to lose my senses
I want to smash things up
And tear down fences.
I want to go away forever
From where I should be
Take me down, lock me out
Then obliterate that key.

"I'm running a marathon
That I never volunteered for

I swim against the tide
And I can't see the shore.
I want to cry, I'd like to die
I'd like to change my name
So take me down, I want to run
I can no longer take the strain.

"I'd like to be hypnotised, anaesthetised
I want to obliviate my brain
Please paralyse or comatise
Come friendly angels kill this pain.
I want to fly away forever
I was king I've lost my crown
There's just a scream in my head
Take me down, take me down, down, down."

Everyday Hero has left Sam about midday. He
would kiss his little hand then take what might
be his last look. But at the same time knowing
that he had already but gone. As the days
passed, poor Sam visibly shrank away. He would
then make his way to Dulwich to see Selsey. The
nurses always informed him of any change,
however small. They all liked her and nicknamed
her The Wonderful. Before leaving at three thirty pm
as before, he would stoop down, brings his lips
to her ear so close as to be a kiss, and everyday
the same thing.

"One day you will wake up
A warm sun will be shining
The birds will be singing in the trees
Bees will be swarming in the flowers
Butterflies will colour the air

159

And little puffy white clouds
Will be sailing across a bright blue sky
And then you will be happy
Happy as a four-year-old with a new hat."

As he spoke the words, her eyes would race as
in dreaming but never would they open and
reveal the bright green deeps that always shone
therein.

On the seventh day Hero is about to repeat his little
farewell ritual. Selsey who had been lying there
in her usual motionless silence, suddenly rises
from the bed, arms outstretched, hands clawing
at the air as if trying to grasp some unseen thing.
Her mouth open in a way as to indicate savage
pain, like a speared fish. She then lets out a high
pitched scream, so high as to be scarcely audible.
Then, slowly sinks back down to the impenetrable
stillness of coma. Hero's blood curdles with fear
and shock, but the nurses have heard it and come
running. Hero slips away leaving the hospital shaken
white and trembling.

At the park, he finds things strangely subdued.
Albert is sitting in his office without the light on, lost
behind the gloom and clutter of his desk. "Sit down
Johnny, I 'av got wery bad news for you. The
osbitawl as just wung to tewll me that Sammy's
'eart has stopped beating at fwee firty and were
unable to get it going again. An' wewl, 'e 'as
passed on like...and er died. They said it was 'is
bwain wot dunnit, and it was inevitable fwom
the beginning, and thass a fack, oh yer.

It's awl a wery gweat twagedy, wery gweat indeed.
As if it aint enough livin in a countwy wots run by
Mickey Mouse and Long John Silver. You 'av got awl
'ell come dan on your 'ed. I always won'ed a boy
called Sam and to lose 'im is a wery bitter an' painful
blow, oh yer."

But Hero's head is still in the bottle
His poor life his sleeping wife
To him it's all a mystery
Why this unkind savagery of life.
To arrange a funeral is a hill he cannot climb
The very thought won't fit his mind
Ideas have no cohesion in the bottle
That strength he just cannot find.

June sits in her high street glory
Pink land of leather paradise
So warm and sweet and cosy
But oh so sadly lacking spice.
But there's soon a knocking at the door
It's Hero with his sorrows and trouble
He pours out his confusion
And that he feels his head is in a bubble.
When he breaks the news on Sam
June says, "Oh that's all my fears,"
Just for a moment is composed
Then lost in floods of tears.
Hubby quickly goes for the cabinet
"We could all do with a drink
Yes, yes a toast to Selsey
It just may help my head to think."
Soon after the third shot
Hero protests, "No, please no more!"

He's hardly eaten for a week
Spins round and crashes to the floor
They talk into the small hours
They're eating sandwiches with tea
June says, "As for the funeral
Don't worry, leave all that to me."

"Thank you June, but there are a few things."

# 58

## Where Snowdrops Cheer

"Pray don't burn him please
Lay him by a grassy bank
Beneath some sturdy trees.
Bury him on the north side
Where Polaris cannot hide
Watchful from the starry sky
With his ever constant eye.
Let snowdrops cheer the winters grim
With lolling heads smile down at him
As time brings its ever ebbing tide
Brief perfection be there side by side.
Then on his stone please carve
Here rests little Sam, we mourn
His sun struck down soon after dawn
He will not fade or die
Unless those who love him pass him by."

It's a very sad day
Not all funerals are sad of course
Hero is standing in a small hexagonal chapel
It has slim gothic windows on five sides
Where the sun lights the interior
But there is no sun, just an awful gloom.
Resting on a small cast iron stand
In the centre of the parquetry marble floor
There is a little gleaming white coffin
A brass plate bears the names
Samuel Brian Smith.

He gazes down at it bewildered
Reads the inscription over and over again
It all seems so unreal, even the names
His mind is still in the bottle.

# 59

## November Light

Suddenly a small door opens
And five girls enter the chapel
They are obviously of Caribbean descent
All are clothed identically
Mauve dresses that sweep to the floor
With pretty white lace collars
And broad purple sashes tied beneath their bosoms
Their patent leather shoes are outdone
By their hair that tumbles down in glossy jet ringlets
That glint with a deep ravishing incandescence.
Even in the seeping November light
They give Hero a slightly shy smile
With their flashing eyes and full mouths
Lavishly decorated with vermillion lipstick.
They form a crescent at the head of the coffin
Stand silent for a few moments
Beautiful in their fuchsia glory
Untouchable in their radiant sanctuary.
Glowing like Pre-Raphaelite angels
They begin to sing in perfect harmony
All things bright and beautiful
And in an instant Hero is back in his classroom
The wonderful tune, the familiar words
Soon sweep him into tears.
They then place their fingertips on the coffin
One at the head, two either side
Their manicured and varnished fingernails
Stand out in vivid relief against the white
Like the petals of a broken daisy
They then sing a delightful little hymn.

# 60

## Be An Angel

Here I am your saviour
I am the way, the light
Hold my hand, I'm Jesus
Your way will then be bright.
Across the sky in Heaven
Another star will shine
Tonight you'll be an angel
And you will be mine.

As the last phrases of the hymn
Swirl up to the top of the chapel
And reverberate away for ever
The girls leave with a few repressed giggles
And all returns to silence.
Hero's head slowly drains to clarity
As if he had taken a large dose of lithium
The bubble has at last broken
He feels strangely well again.
One spark of embryonic joy
There just may be a path out of hell
The service was a quiet affair
There was almost no one there.
Selsey's mother had missed the train
And her sister, what a shame
June had sobbed, quite overcome
Hubby wisely took her home.
Only our brave Hero stayed
To see poor Sammy in his grave
On Sam's going I'll no longer dwell
There is just this last farewell.

# 61

## **Promise To Sam**

"Well Sam it's time to say goodbye
And I must do this awful thing
I have to leave you where you lie
You my love, my friend and joy
My only sweet and lovely boy.
You were the sun that always shone
The precious tune to our life song
I'll shed no more tears, tears are cheap
For you I'll let the angels weep.
Fond memories of your life so brief
Now all tainted with my grief
Sammy if you but only knew
How very wise, how very true.
Your sweet little nursery rhyme
When clouds fall down and rain
It's best to kick them up again
But these clouds I cannot kick
My wounds are not the sort to lick
I'll save the love I can't give you
For your mother twice and true
Twice and true, that's my promise to you."

Hero slowly turns to go, but where?
Joy, his answer is right there
Two little ladies dressed all in black
And complete with titfa tat
At the sight of poor Sammy's coffin
They both begin a wailing sobbing.
"Oh God has set his little heart free

Poor boy, it should have really been me."
"It's no use crying we can't stay."
Then gently steers them on their way
Well the dear old ladies in a way
They've both bought food and saved the day.
Back at the house that's like a shed
The ladies set the quaintest spread
Now that Hero's cleared his head
His stomach is in great need of being fed
With eager eyes he views the spread
Never a funeral breakfast to compare
But certainly there is good share.

## 62

### Breakfast In A Bag

Sardine sandwiches already made
Half a dozen cans of lemonade
Assorted nuts and dried apricots
Peas pudding and grilled faggots.
Salad in a bag, tomatoes on the vine
Danish blue, cheddar cheese and parsnip wine
A small joint of smoked ham
And two pots of homemade jam.
Black pudding, corned beef and mustard
Apple pie and two tins of custard
Crispy rolls and half a pound of butter
Sweets and chocolate raisins amid the table's clutter
Large cups of tea as many as you can take
With ginger biscuits and Battenburg cake.

Yes indeed it was a very, very sad day
But the ladies soothed the sting away
When asked why they'd lost their way
"The silly timetables changed on Saturday."
What have I told you about Saturday?
It's a day when all things can go astray
Then after they'd had another weep
Sat by the fire and soon fast asleep.

They both stayed for two more days
And gave the house a woman's touch
But the strain of seeing Selsey
Just proved a little bit too much.

So Hero's left his heart to burn
Until days of smiles at last return.

It's the seventh day of December
Today Sammy would be five
It's a great day for celebration
Even though he's not alive.
Gleeful nurses smile profusely
Oh she's back it's good news
No one has told her of poor Sam
Sadly it's a job they all refuse.

It's a very strange encounter
Like her returning from the dead
She looks dew fresh and beautiful
Just calmly sitting on the bed.
Hero's stuck for words to tell
But she waves them all aside
There's just a single teardrop
For strong feelings she can't hide.

# 63

## The Light

"Say nothing of poor Sam, I know I know!
Though I have been locked in limbo
I saw him standing in the garden
By the running water beneath the shining bow

"I could hear your every word
But my eyes were some other place
I saw bright angels with him
And his sweet and mended face.

"I was bathed in such a light
Completely devoid of stress and strain
But sadly now I have returned
My desperate heart is full of pain.

"I've seen a strange and hypnotic world
Of Heaven and God's golden light
To wake to this bleak winter
A gross shock of grey and white.

"That happy light's still with me
A better light will never burn
It was a place of enchanted time
And by the grace of God I may return."

"Come sit beside me on the bed
Oh how I've thirsted for your touch
It's in this special moment
That our love can mean so much.

Oh Johnny you look so awful
You've surely lost a stone
Now tell me all about it
It's a time that I can't own."

"Oh Sesley, it was very bitter."

# 64

## Last Blades Of Hope

"Bitter is not the lemon juice that finds the cut
Not the east wind that sweeps the January streets
Bitter is not the loss of fortune
No, bitter is more than the loss of possession.
Fear and loneliness is a dreadful mix
It's then the mind plays awful tricks
All fight departed, oh how I fell
I saw the burning edge of hell.
I ran but I was at the desert's sand
Where the last blades of hope snapped in my hand
I walked the cool corridors of purgatory
I called for help, there was no answer
I thought they would come, not a soul appeared
I looked in all places and found no God
Oh Selsey, how bitter that was!
Oh how I tried to move that painful mountain
But no strength flowed from my mental fountain
They said it was a matter of time, Sam will die
Could I but stop the sun still in the sky?
It was the gathering of all my fears
And bought a pain too deep, too blunt for tears."

## 65

### To Burn The Nerve

"One dull depressing afternoon
The duty nurse took me to a room
She said, 'We never do admit,
But most of these just won't make it.'
The children played in groups and sang
Oblivious of the sword that hung
The nurses there were sweet and calm
But the kids outshone them with their charm.
Bravely smiling come and go
Like little angels dressed in snow
Bright upturned faces full of trust
So innocently trusting us.
One little girl she spoke to me
She said, 'Tomorrow I'll be three.
But in the night she took her wings
How do the nurses bear such things?
It burnt the nerve and numbed the pain
So I couldn't feel that way again."

"Please no more Johnny
I'm so tired and my heart is frail and sad
We have to climb a mountain
That's a job that must be done
Before we can get back our lives
That was so much joy and fun."

Selsey lays down and closes her eyes
"Kiss me Johnny and do that thing again."
"What thing?"
"You know I heard it everyday
Come on say it to me
It's just like the Lord's Prayer."

# 66

## Green Shoots

"One day you will wake up
A warm sun will be shining
The birds will be singing in the trees
Bees will be swarming the flowers
Butterflies will colour the air
And little fluffy white clouds
Will be sailing across a bright blue sky
And then you will be happy
Happy as a four-year-old with a new hat."

"Oh that's so lovely Johnny, so lovely."
He kisses her and rubs her thighs
And the sandman takes her away.

That smile, her shimmering light
Is still unharmed and burning bright
Her deep beauty still intact
Those eyes still brightly shone
But the effervescent girly girl
Sad to say has completely gone.

# 67

## **<u>Hopefulness</u>**

Pull out the stops, throw in everything
This mountain we shall climb
However steep or slippery
We can do it, just given time.
Storm clouds have lifted all darkness gone
Heralds fair winds and weather
A chance at last to grasp a life
Once thought had gone forever.
Now gather the broken pieces
And build a force that's worth beholding
And race to gain those sweeter days
Of pleasant dreams unfolding.

# 68

## To Kill A Mountain

The mountain rose from the lush pastures
Its twin peaks glittered in the morning light
Looking glorious and deceptively calm
We were all high with optimism
Five men and three girls.
When you need to climb a mountain
It takes passion, brawn and brain
So you just be damn careful
You may not get the chance again.

I woke in pre-dawn at 12°C below
Venus hung gem like between the peaks
That rose luminous from the jet
An awesome sight of crushing beauty
Sufficient to enrich one's life for ever.
When you're on a mountain
Your presence desecrates its peace
So always do remember
You're up there on a lease.

The weather changed on the third day
A big wind roared down between the peaks
Savaging us as we tried to gain height
One climber slipped, another tried to catch him
Both fell with serious results.
It takes skill to climb a mountain
So listen to experienced advice
And keep it tucked inside your head
You may not get it twice.

The chopper arrived before dark
The man that was blown over broke his leg
His mate dislocated his shoulder
The chopper took them and their girls
So we then had ample food.
If you wrestle with a mountain
Be sure there's nothing that you lack
For you can be quite certain
That the mountain will fight back.

Next day's climb, a joyless slog through clouds
Ice rain, impalpable greyness and fear
As the rock rose steep and sinister above
It was a desperate time, but we won
We reached the snowline and blue sky.
You can cheer when you are winning
But you never can be sure
It's just when you think you've made it
That the mountain has one trick more.

It was heavenly, we were drenched in light
Wonderful views and warm sunshine
Our one remaining girl got snow blindness
She was so overcome by looking
So she and her partner could go no further.
If you pit your strength against a mountain
Get your wisdom in advance
One or two mistakes too many
You won't get a second chance.

Nearing the summit we lost our way
The route became dangerous for a novice
So the leader went ahead to reconnoitre
Pick, pick, pick, out of sight and sound

179

I thought he fell, he did, I was alone.
It takes time to climb a mountain
What they said was true
If you try to kill a mountain
There's a chance it may kill you.

Selsey came home for Christmas
But still sadly very frail
Her sleepy days and fitful night
They do make a sorry tale.
We had an invite from Albert
To spend our Christmas there
At his rustic hilltop cottage
By Horniman's garden amid the rushing air.

It's quite inimitable, a paradise unchallenged.
On summer evenings, when the warm air comes
rolling up the hill, Albert will sit smoking his pipe,
the rocking chair creaking on the terrace cobbles.
His grey cat ever present, "'ees a wery untidy
cweature indeed, and thass a fack." He will be
gazing over his tumbling cottage garden, crammed
full with every imaginable flower.
Twisting paths and precipitous steps between endless
potted shrubs of all shapes and hues, but they are
outnumbered by a myriad of hanging baskets swinging
from vine covered arches and trellis work, making
mobility hazardous. Spending equally endless hours
watering, clipping and dead-heading, up and down
forever, but just as often falling asleep in his rocking
chair. "I am a wery lucky man to 'av such a place to
live and die in, wery lucky indeed, wiv a sunset
everwy day of the year, lucky indeed oh yer." For a
few weeks of the year it's a neo-Mediterranean

suntrap, but it's winter now and the wind whistles over the roof and buffets the house like the sails of a sea going yacht. Inside its cosy and the kettle sings on the range.

# 69

## Xmas On The Hill

Selsey just adores the place
Its presence brings her close to tears
For cherished childhood memories
Of her sweet and pampered years.

Red brick steps lead to a porch
Enclosing an oak studded door
With its bottle glass lenticel
Brings a promise of something more.

Once inside you're in a cosy room
That could be called the hall
Graced by a comely inglenook
Oak beams and panels all.

The open fire in the inglenook
Well that's very seldom burning
But Albert thinks today is special
It's a day of Christmas yearning.

The Christmas dinner went very well
Correct unto the letter
So why bother to describe it
When Dickens did it so much better.

Now evening tea with hot sausage rolls
And a mountain of hot mince pies
All made in house, wow!
That was a pleasant surprise.

Albert wasn't short on sermons
And consumed a lot of port
As the evening did progress
I feared he may say more than he ought.

But he didn't; he was quite profound. Referring
to Selsey he says, "The 'uman 'art and sowl is
fwagile an' wery easily bwoken, oh yer! But the
bwain is igorwant and often wery wiolent and
stoopid too. I 'av just wed this book Owigin of
the species. Now it's wery plain to see that
Charles Darwin was a pwophit oo was sent by
God to show the 'owl wewld the marvels of its
cweation and 'ow ee dunnit. Igorwant people
say that 'ee 'as kiwlled God, wewl, ee aint.
Until Darwin come up wiv a foo monkeys of 'is
own , then it's awl dan to almighty God, oh yer
and thass a fack!"

God safely reinstated in his rightful place, we must
now plough on through the bitter winter months and
see about that mountain we have to climb. But things
aren't good.

# 70

## **Of Caustic Tears**

"It's months now since Sammy's gone
How I've got by I'll never know
Grief is such a waste of time
Life's clock so painfully slow.
As wasteful days drift by
All I want to do is sleep
And when I drag myself from torpor
All I seem to do is weep.
Sammy's room it haunts me
Things are left just as they lay
Untouched since that dread morning
As we then both rushed away.
Outside his trike lays on its side
Close by his rabbit hutch
His bat and ball there in the shed
With other things we dare not touch.
So this feeling still hangs on
And I see no sign of spring
All through this dreadful winter
Johnny Hero's been my everything.
It's the little things that hurt so much
That go rolling back the years
A small toy found in some corner
Fills my heart with caustic tears.
I don't think I shall get better
Not before I clear it all away
But I really haven't got the steel
So for now that's where things stay.
His framed photo on the kitchen wall

I kiss it a dozen times a day
Maybe I should hide it
Then this pain may go away.
For it clouds my living day
Then follows me to bed
Whenever I wake in the night
I feel that I am dead.
They tell me time heals everything
But I don't know if it will
For every morning that I wake
The pain is deep, it's red, it's shrill."

Through the long winter they both looked to the spring in a naive hope that all will be well. But spring is often a reluctant visitor. Hero has always been alert to Selsey's ups and downs. He would tell her happy little stories to cheer her and paint verbal pictures not always with the desired results.

## 71

## Keep To The B Roads

"When summer comes
We'll hire a camper van
Leave early in the morning
See flower gardens and castles
Stop at picturesque old villages
And eat cream teas just any time
Keep to the B roads.

"We'll drive down sunny lanes
To the seaside and the West
Live on Cornish pasties
With salty chips and tomato sauce
Scoff dolly mixtures and sherbet serenades
Fall asleep in the grass just any time
And keep to the B roads."

"Oh stop the baby stuff, Johnny."

"I'll frequent you with love my angel
Lay you down by clear waters
Wear nothing but your summer dress
I'll kiss your pansy just any time
And keep to the B roads."

She smiles, but it's a smile to cover tears.

**72**

## The Dandypuffs

In her troubled dreaming night
When silver memories flicker bright
Her broken heart and burnt out soul
Of what liniment could make it whole?
Take the egg that's smashed asunder
What hand on Earth could mend the plunder?
That shattered wine glass once sparkled bright
No glue could scarce redeem its plight.

In her painful lonely night
That dreadful vision comes in sight
Her damaged mind, her broken brain
Pray what therapy to right it all again.
Could God above mend in a day?
That perfect dandypuff once blown away
Well I'm afraid to say the answer's no
But given time, another one may grow.

So time we will give her but I can promise you nothing
So let's fly forward on the magic wings of time, two
years!

# 73

## The First Crocus

Spring has crept into the park
Brings the bird song crystal sharp
With it comes her eternal blessing
Trees and shrubs in fresh green dressing.
April's here, it's rained all night
But the morning sun is warm and bright
Soft breezes blow and bring warm air
The barometer swings from change to fair.
In the sunshine vapours rising
From the soil sweet scent it's prising
All seems well at Peckham Rye
The wind has brought an azure sky.
Spring bulbs are present to start the race
Crocus and daffodils show their ever pleasant face.

In the top nursery Hero rests on his shovel
And contemplates the weeds and trouble
But he is diverted, there's a flapping up above
Just like the sound of a giant dove.
Yes, it is a huge bird tangled in a tree
He quickly clambers up to set the creature free
It isn't very easy, the bird is in a wild struggle
The twine that ensnares it is an awful muddle.
Free at last, but Hero falls and drops like lead
On his descent to earth he knocks his head
He lays there on his back, KO'd for sure
I'll tell you now there are strange things in store.
Barely conscious he lays there for a rest
But he's aware the bird is on his chest

Large as a buzzard, perky as a magpie
And viewing Hero with her amber eye.
She then sings a song of great enchantment
And in the song he hears the words
"You are young and handsome
And I will pay you any ransom
Just anything that you request
You set me free it's my bequest."
Though dazed our Hero puzzles this
Then in a moment makes a wish
"I have a television that is monochrome
I must say that I would like a coloured one
My wife and I would like to view
A television with colours bright and true."

The bird again begins to speak to him
With a clear voice of an Indian hill minor.

"Your wish be granted right away
You will have your set this very day
Now you may need me many times
Just whistle down the wind five times
Two short and three long
And I'm bound by God to hear your song."

Then she rises like a kite
Is soon lost in a sea of light
But that shining sea of light
Slowly turns grey, then into night.
In his head a throbbing pain
Then slowly light, then dark again
Hears strange voices overhead
Feels he's moving on a bed
Then wakes to find he's in a chair

Familiar faces all about, they stare.

"Wot in 'ells name 'as 'appened to you Johnny? That
is a wery nasty gash you got on your 'ed. I wondered
wot the 'ell 'ad come over you when you don't come
back for a break like, then find you laying on the
gwound
'arf dead. I will get the twactor dwiver to take you back
'ome. You aint in no fit state to work, oh yer. I've
made you a cup of tea, an' 'ere's a cupawl of
pennycilian tablets for you. I won't be needin' nuffin
where I'm goin' and thass a fack, as you know, I'm a
wery ill man oh yer."

He's soon home, to bed and sleep
Selsey's watching television but later has a peep
At breakfast in the morning
He tells her of the magic bird.
"Rubbish! That's the daftest thing I've ever heard
Johnny Hero I don't believe you, I'm sorry
Don't kid me, it's off the back of a lorry."

Things are no better in the evening
When they're having tea
"How I hate dishonest people
Why aren't you straight with me?
I know the price of flat screens
I've seen them in the store
They're far beyond our budget
At a thousand pounds or more."

# 74

## I Want A Sequin Dress

As the days turn into weeks
He sees less and less of her
Her life is centred round the telly
It's become a thing she does prefer.
She's constantly disgruntled
And says, "Life just isn't fair
All those people winning money
Oh how I want to be right there.
Oh how I'd love to go out dancing
In a gorgeous sequin dress
And meet up with celebrity
Then be interviewed by press."
She's quite often very distant
And behaves as if he wasn't there
And just as often brooding
About problems she won't share.
If she isn't glued to the flat screen
She's on the phone to mum
It's a sad thing I must tell you
There's even worse to come.

Coming home from work one day
There's the pungent smell of burning hay
Smoke flames and a great garden fire
Selsey's beating out her suppressed desire.
The rabbit hutch with Sammy's bed
His toys and contents of the shed
Every little treasure burning
To satisfy her bright new yearning.

"Selsey darling, what are you doing?
The place looks such a dreadful ruin."
"So! It's no use living in the past
This dull nostalgia cannot last
The flat screen telly is in Sammy's room
It was becoming like a tomb
With a sofa and drinks bar
It's now my private cinema
This place is really far too small
I'd like an upstairs and a hall.
If I really had my way
I'd put this bloody prefab with the hay."
"So that's what you think about my house!"
"Our house!"
"Then I'll see my magic bird."
"Bullshit Johnny, bullshit you stupid nerd."

Hero's in the top nursery again
Thinking what he's doing surely is insane
And his brains are feeling odd
"Is it magic or am I grappling with God?"
He whistles and whistles, then whistles again
Still gazing to the sky, is it all in vain?
But the song of great enchantment
And as before he hears the words
"You are still young and handsome
And I will pay you precious ransom."
She floats down from the treetop
For her just one effortless hop
Such daunting presence such graceful line
And she's been eyeing me all the time.

"Now tell me, what ails you?
What troubles you dear friend?

Please have no fear good fellow
There's no problem I can't mend."

"My wife she's so unhappy
That makes me sad as well
Where all her delusions come from
It's most difficult to tell.
She no longer wants my prefab
But a house with upstairs and down
Close by the railway station
So she can quickly get to town."

"Is that all you ask of me?
I Sharheen the ruler of the sky
Your wish be granted right away
Houses, they're not in short supply.
Now I have chicks in the nest
Time is crucial, no time to wait,"
Glides slowly through the arboretum
Like the insidious shadow of fate.

At the hut, Albert is in a high state of excitement
"I see this big black bird this mornin' I aint never
see the likes before. It must 'av escaped fwom a
zoo. It was bigger than an eagawl, oh yer an' thass
a fack!"
Back home Selsey's in a similar state
She's jumping up and down with joy
At last a proper house, oh boy.
"In my hand I have a letter
That shall make my life much better
They want the prefab and the land
And give us money in our hand.
Kingston properties will build ten units here

And they will pay us very dear
Two hundred thousand is the price
Or swap a house all done up nice.
I've been to view it at two today
Said we'd sign the contract right away
It's a dream come true I've always had
Just think going upstairs to bed
Oh zing! A house with up and down
By the railway into town."

Hero looks about him at his love worn prefab
But sees his mother and his father
And all the work they did for him.
"Dad rebuilt this top to bottom
Bathroom, loo and kitchen sink
To move from here's a massive leap
The thought has pushed me to the brink.
Please calm down Selsey give me time
I must have a little time to think."
"To think? To think?!!
What do you need to think about
You good for nothing dreamer
You're so negative, you make me shout."
"But Selsey, this is an historic building
Built by the yanks in nineteen forty-four
It should have a conservation order
Then it would soon be worth much more."
"Johnny you're just talking rubbish
It's nothing but a flat pack shack
And if your dad was still alive
He'd have a job to get his money back.
And you still want time to think
The only thing that's historic is your brain
And stop becoming such a pain

Oh you stupid wimpish fool
You push me much too far."
Screams with fury, slams the door
And sobs inside her private cinema
"Bloody hell! Curse the day that I was born,"
Then wanders off and mows the lawn
But her moods and fury won't subside
For poor Hero there's no place to hide
So after days and days of hell
He sees she never will retract
No heart to fight her, he then relents
And goes to sign the fatal contract.

Very shortly after moving in
To the house that's all done up nice
There's an awful lot of trouble
In sweet domestic paradise.
The van man that lives next door
"Ay, you move that on right now
Don't park it there I said
Shut ya gob ya mouffy cow."
The couple on the other side
I'm afraid they were no joke
With their eternal barbeques
That filled the place with smoke.
One evening Selsey throws a rage
With the garden hose she kills it with a stroke
The poor couple they exploded
But for their efforts got a soak.
Then a neighbour raising shouting match
The van man on Selsey's side
But after massive altercation
The wet couple did subside.
For Hero things were brittle

x

195

With all that banging on his head
And oh how he rues the day
He sold the house that's like a shed.
Indoors there's worse to come
It all soon becomes a travesty
Shag pile carpets cover every floor
The hall the bath the lavatory.
That interior decor, oh dear
Wallpapers of truly hideous design
Although June across the way
She thinks it's quite divine.
There's no more home coming smiles
Gone the sweet rosy bower
She's forever giving orders
And exercising woman's power.
"Take ya muddy boots off
You're enough to make me cry
Every time you come here
You bring half the mud in Peckham Rye.
Wash your grimy hands
You're marking all the paint
With someone like you around
I need to be a flaming saint."
The house is filled with gaudy furniture
Mostly gilt and shocking pink
Together with the wallpaper
It could make your pupils shrink.
And there's the coup de gras
"This is not the house that's like a shed
So with all these upper rooms
I think I'll have a separate bed."
"Selsey where did you get the money?"
"Oh, five grand on the card of course."
"Pray what is this card?"

"A credit card you silly horse"
"Does everybody have a card?"
"Yes, that's how they pay of course
Everybody has one darling."
"Good God... do they?"

The wet people they're more trouble
They just love their heavy metal
That throbs away all day and night
And even shakes the kitchen kettle.
How to stop this painful racket
Selsey's missed it by a mile
Every time she pleads with them
She just gets a benign smile.

One evening Hero's lost in thought
And hears his Selsey calling
"Come up into my bedroom darling,"
And what he sees is quite appalling.
"How do you like this swim suit?"
"It's appealing, and er appalling."
"I thought you'd like to see me
And the joys of its revealing."
"Oh Sel, you look just miraculous
It gives me that old feeling."
Then he kisses her profusely
And soon his silly head is reeling.
Some time later they're sitting up
In her bed of pink and gilt
She's smiling up into his eyes
To cover the delusion she has built.
"Oh Johnny I love you muchly
But please do one tiny thing for me
Get me out of this place

And set my crumpled spirit free.
I'm sick of this close suburbia
It really isn't very nice
With all this eternal aggravation
It's very far from paradise.
I loathe those horrid little people
They have nothing in their head
And for all their lack of enterprise
They may as well be dead.
Why do they love that crappy music?
And I am very sure
They think that life on Earth began
In nineteen sixty-four."

## 75

## <u>If Only I Had</u>

"I want a house up on a hill
Where all London lays beneath
I'm sure I'll feel much better
Living up there on Blackheath.
Find me a Victorian villa
With carriage entrance doors
Two thirty foot reception rooms
Graced with polished hardwood floors.
With five romantic bedrooms
That also vary in their size
And a sunny long walled garden
That for you would be a prize.
I want to mix with artists
And do the quirky things they do
Like writing four line poems
While sitting on the loo.
I really want a music room
And a library and study too
Darling sweetness if you love me
Don't tease me with that bird
For anyone with half a brain
Must know that's quite absurd."

Well Selsey Carnival that was pretty cheap
But I suppose you had to choose
Between living in a hell hole
Or your contrived deceitful ruse!

Hero's standing in the nursery

And he's feeling pretty high
"Oh good riddance to that dreadful place,"
As he whistles to the sky.
He waits there gazing wistfully
Into the clear midsummer skies
And after what seems an eternity
The descending bird he spies.
Soon the song of great enchantment
And in the song he hears the words
"You are still young and handsome
I will pay you goodly ransom."
"Oh Sharheen I am in trouble
I curse the day I wed
She gives me cold bum and breakfast
And no longer shares my bed.
She's upset all the neighbours
My life's become a lonely pain
I'm begging you for something
To bring her love to me again.
She says she wants a Victorian villa
With a long garden and a view
Please say no more good fellow
I know just the thing for you."
"I Sharheen the great
Shall always rule the sky
Unless my powers are abused
It's written I'll not die.
Your wish it will be granted
That ransom shall be paid
But I beg of you be prudent
Because for that I really am afraid."

She spreads her glorious glossy black wings
Then glides across the nursery
Lifts effortlessly over the trees

Catches the warm thermals
And is soon lost in the shining silvery sky
Surely the dark angel of destiny.

"It aint no use looking up there Johnny,"
It's Albert; always a rare caller.
"There's a wery smart young man in the office
dwessed in a black soot and a wed tie
Says 'ees fwom Kingston Pwoperties and wants
to 'av a word wiv you ee said about your new
owse, wery urgent"

He's looking pretty self-important
And as sweet as Grecian honey
As often is the case
When spending other people's money.
"Your house on Railways Cuttings sir
We'd like to buy it off you
We need it very urgently
And will pay you twice its value.
I have a deal in mind for you
Four hundred thousand is our price
Considering your house is just a terrace
You won't need to think about it twice."
"Well it isn't just money I want."
"I could make it half a million sir
Or I could arrange another swap
That's whatever you prefer
We're desperate for an access road
So we need your house in hand
We're building two hundred units on the railway land.
But if you'd like a Victorian house sir
I have this villa on Blackheath
It's in a very desirable position
Where all London lays beneath.

Totally detached with carriage entrance doors
Two beautiful reception rooms
With tropical hardwood floors.
Here's the keys just have a shoofty
Take your wife, just you two
Let me know first thing tomorrow
This deal must be pushed through.
So that's half a million pounds
Or we could exchange your house sir
Just show your wife around
Choose the deal you both prefer."

But Hero says too much
He mentions that half a million
Selsey yells out, "Take the cash,"
And goes jumping to the ceiling
Soon she's quite hysterical
And cannot absorb the other deal
"Just take the bloody money!"
She screams out loud and shrill
"Now calm down Selsey dearest
And don't you be a silly cow
You asked for a Victorian villa
Well you come and see it now."

Selsey gazes through the French windows
At a lawn with buttercups and clover
"This garden is quite enchanting,"
I think she's been won over.
"This place is so incredible,"
And when the kitchen is produced
"Oh, deliriously beautiful"
And she's instantly seduced.

**76**

## Extreme Beauty

My friend she has a bonsai
A thousand pounds it cost, and only two feet high
It's so extremely beautiful
Enough to make a timber merchant cry.

In the dreaming hearts of little girls
There lurks a fairy queen
She is extremely beautiful
And ever craving to be seen.

Please don't rage plain ladies
The unbeautiful sigh no more
For when the fairy's grown up
She can be a frightful bore.

Now don't you be too hard on her
Extreme beauty comes at a cost
She's often thrown in the cauldron
And by forty all is lost.

It isn't just the fair sex
That is savaged by a dream
There's that bright eyed Mr Nobody
Whose brains aren't what they seem.

Motor cars! An awful cause of sin
Glossy stream-lined body extravagance of line
Oh, she's so extremely beautiful
EUREKA! This car it must be mine.

Cash the shares, remortgage the house
Already dangerously high
Eight ports of fire and smoking wheels
Just take me to the sky!

But we all adore things beautiful
So where does the madness lie?
It's plain to see, it's simple
In the brain and in the eye.

Selsey picks up a pile of bills
She gives them scant regard
To her they're just a trifle
And pays them with the card.
They're only rates and service bills
Nothing to compare with antique furnishing
Oh the price of oriental rugs
And the luxuries she's been purchasing.
The speed she has been spending
By the time she bought the lot
I'm sure her little plastic card
Was getting very, very hot.

## 77

## Trouble In Paradise

Again there's trouble with the neighbours
Because she seldom sees them
So often in their second home
Or won't talk for some odd reason.
Only yesterday she met one
She was walking to the station
And even when politely pursued
She would not engage in conversation.
Selsey's getting bored and lonely
And will not get herself a job
She's like the snooty crow next door
And has now become a snob.
She thinks maybe it is because
She isn't middle class
In truth it's when the wind blows
That she's showing half her arse.
So a small fortune on posh clothing
Then struts about like a prissy toff
Mimicking those starchy trouts
That act as if they've never blown off.

Hero's getting desperate about the rising debt
And tries to lecture her on money
That often ends in tears
Or else she thinks it's very funny.

# 78

## **Too Many Gadgets**

"You have two wardrobes full of dresses
And cupboards full of shoes
And a multitude of gadgets
That I've never seen you use."
"Oh poohy, I hate all your economy
I've just bought a four by four
So I can shop in style
In safe comfort door to door.
And don't you buy me any sell-by dates
It's a thing I do abhor
Those wretched yellow labels
I find them sticking to the floor.
And as for cut price wine
That will never quench my thirst
And stop whingeing about money
Or my bloody head will burst."

So financial crisis hopeless
While she has that little card
But as Albert's always saying
"Married life is wery 'ard.
An' when it comes to cards
You don't never know wot can turn up
Littawl gewls that look as sweet as unny
or the 'oly lamb of Gawd itself, can gwow up
like a bweeding wowlf while uvvers will turn
out like lambs that are both 'armless and usefull
oh yer!"

So flush in her glitzy rags
And armed with her four by four
Every day she leaves the house
Through her carriage entrance door.
She makes her way to Greenwich
Which she finds a tiresome bind
However diligent her search is
Not a single parking place to find.
That doesn't bother her much
She just parks it on the line
So for every zealous warden
She's an easy glass of wine.
And as for those damn tickets
Pops them in the Aga or the paper bin
They won't intimidate me
And I'll not be worrying
You see she's on an urgent quest
For culture and some learning
To find the intellectual set
It's her very latest yearning.
It's a guess how intellectual they are
But I think she's made a find
In her brief acquaintance with them
They've done something to her mind.

Today she got up very early
Dressed in a purple leotard
Stabbing in the air on the hardwood floor
And punching pretty fearful hard.
With every little venomous punch
There is a violent chant
Her face glows flush with perspiration
Like some exotic plant.

**79**

## Too Many Degrees

"I must do more exercise
And run two miles a day
I must eat more wholegrain
Keep that heart attack away.
I must eat more fish and fibre
To improve my brain
I must get in discussions
They must feel the strain.
I must learn from the well informed
And have a vital point of view
And I must be more political
And tell others what to do.
I must go, get a degree
Or maybe even two
I think I want to study law
And have important work to do."

Hero comes downstairs woken by all the noise
He can't stop laughing at what he sees
"How about a bit of breakfast Sel?"
Selsey carries on punching
"Don't stop me this is important!
If you want to make yourself into a slob
Eating fatty breakfasts, go ahead
But don't you include me!"

"I will not be crushed I will not be crushed
I must be more political I must be more political."

When Albert is told of this, his face is full of frown.

"Wot did I keep tellin' ya Johnny
Never put ya wife on a pedestawl, now she
'as started acting like a clown. I don't know
what you 'av done to that poor gewl, but it
do sound like wery dangerous beavya. In all
my days on this erff, I aint never encantered
a cwushed woman. In my 'umble opinion
women are abart as cwushable as an Indian
wubba bawl. And as for being politicawl, wewl,
Adolf 'itler was a politician an' Starlin and a lotta
uvva wery nasty people, and thass a fack, oh yer!"

On returning home that night
The intellectuals if you please
And a lot of other hanger-ons
Have called around for wine and cheese.
There's no dinner on the go
Just an awful lot of wine
Very little bread and cheese
And Selsey looks besotted by a handsome swine.
"Oh Johnny darling, this is Leo
Isn't he just simply divine?
Do mix around with my new friends
And get yourself some wine."
It's true that Leo's very cool
With an extra overload of charm
Takes a lively interest in Hero
And he really does disarm.
He's an ex-officer in the SAS
A curator at the observatory
A collector of fine art
And has a masters in astronomy.

He owns a racy blue Bugatti
And they say that it's a fast one
He becomes our Selsey's guru
And nicknamed her Dolly Parton.
The others are a motley crowd
A pilot with a phobia of flying
Two solicitors, one struck off
And a surgeon with a fear of dying.
Leo wants to open the house
As a school of alternative education
That sort of thing is very in
And could be a new sensation.
A different subject every evening
Sunday social, wine and cheese
Mostly music, poetry arts etc
And Selsey she agrees.

Monday art classes on the lawn
Selsey on a pillar in a very classic pose
Thirty men with pencil and paper
And Selsey completely without clothes.
Tuesday there's hands on healing
Oversubscribed a shade too much
With thirty would be artists
That are there for just a touch.
Wednesday a talk on horology by Leo
Which was very well received
Then the pilots on crystal healing
Not surprising no one did believe.
Thursday links between Phrenology and Palmistry
That didn't seem to do much good
Though very earnestly delivered
There's no reason why it should.
Friday poetry, now that's a thing

There was a young lady from Dover
Though very well attended
What a relief when it was over.

There just maybe a shade of truth in what
Albert has to say about poets.
"Poets? Thems wery unsaverwy cawicters indeed, wery
unsaverwy, oh yer! You don't never wanna
git one in ya 'ouse. The sorta person oo never
do no work and spend a lotta time cweepin
abart turnin' the andawls of bedroom doors
wery late at night. And just ang abart wearing
big 'ats and bwite wed scarves, oh yer. But
worse of awl they don't never put anyfing on
paper that is as weedable as 'umpty dumpty
and thass a fack!
They wite pertry like making a
compost 'eap; chuck awl the words in then 'ope
that they wiwll turn into sumfing good. Then
along come a cwitic oo don't know nuffing abart
pertry, and wot aint never witten a poem, an'
weave a lotta magic innit, that wern't never
there in the first place, oh yer!"

As chaotic weeks churn by
Selsey finds the school is boring her
And the house is getting knocked about
And vaguely like the station at Victoria.
2000 pounds on the card for wine
In the cellar stacked up high
But with all the hangers on
Plus the intellectuals have almost drunk it dry.

While Hero labours in the park

It's a rather odd shaped trio
Selsey, she's not often manifest
She's chasing the lights up town with Leo.
Hero comes home worn and tired
To find an empty house, and a letter
What's inside is pretty rich
"Sorry about the mess, run out of everything
Left for Italy with Leo and mater as chaperone
That Leo, isn't he such a gent?
Do tidy up, and don't forget to phone."

She didn't leave her number
Or any date of her returning
Now October's come to the enchanted garden
And the sweet scent of dry leaves burning.

# 80

## <u>Gone But Still About</u>

"My wife went out last August
And I don't think she'll be returning
For what I learned about her
Out was her deepest yearning.
Whenever I came home at night
For some loving and respite
All she ever said was, 'Let's go out',
"She never told me where out was
Or where she'd like to go
It just became a shout
'For God's sake let's go out!'
Now I'm an easy kind of chap
Quite happy here at home
I thought she liked my company
So I had no wish to roam.

"So I never could equate those
Who chased a distant star
And although they have everything
Are never happy where they are.
My wife's a smiley sort of girl
She's ever easy on the eye
And sometimes when I think of her
I feel I want to cry.
In fact I miss her quite a lot
Yes it surely is a tragedy
She was never in my slot
I'm sure if you should meet her
She'll show you all about
For what I get to hear of her
She really has found out!!"

# 81

## A Table To One's Self

Hero's warmed to being single
The blissful lack of eternal rush
Time to watch the dying autumn sun
Submerge London in its crimson flush.
Today the garden's turning gold
The lawn strewn with yellow leaves
Time to search for chestnuts in the park
Beneath the twisted ancient trees.
Sunday Greenwich comes into its own
Strolling families with dolled up mothers
Time to indulge in the eccentric pleasures
Of observing quirks and oddities of others.
Then to patronise the tea house
And have a table all to oneself
Then to look around for others
That may be also on the shelf.

# 82

## Evening Song

Hero's relaxing in his golden garden
And though it's far from hot
He's where the sun falls most of the time
And warms his favourite spot.

He's feeling pleasantly idle
And doesn't think it's wrong
To forget about the clover lawn
And listen to the blackbird's evening song.

"I suppose I ought to clear the lawn
I'd better find the rake,"
But to think this peace is permanent
Is a very big mistake.

A sudden noise comes from the house
Like a symphony out of tune
And in a flash he is quite sure
That he'll be needed pretty soon.

"Johnny! Where are you?!"
Loud clatter on hardwood floors
Desperate wailing and angry shouts
Despairing groan and slamming of doors.
Then cracks the solitude of the garden
"There you are, and sitting down!
Get up now and pay the driver!
I've taken a taxi right across town"

"Do you know how much that cost Sel?!"
"Course I do, it was seventy-four
Well sixty pounds was all I had
You can bet he's feeling pretty sore."

# 83

## The Rake

"Oh Johnny do stop going on
I've had an awful time
And as for that damn Leo
I'd like to incinerate the swine.

Why did I ever believe his tosh?
And I am ashamed to say
I thought I really loved him
No one told me he was gay.

He took a flight to California
And left me high and dry in Rome
With his blasted mater
And no money to get home.

Grand cultural tour of Italy
With his chaperoning mother
All those smooth Italian waiters
He had no eyes for any other.

I'm tired and starving hungry
You take me out to dinner."
"Sorry Sel, only bread and cheese
And just a bottle in the cellar."

They've eaten in the grand kitchen
Hero's giving her a wistful stare
She's looking sweetly sun kissed
The roman sun has bleached her hair.

He gives her a little cuddle of intent
Oh another big mistake
"Get off...you men are all the same."
"Oh well...where did I put that rake?"

Amid the breakfast morning rush
A sad remorseful Selsey does confess
That she paid for the complete tour
"And our finances are in a mess.
"Leo took a loan out on the house
The bank manager was his buddy
In all two hundred thousand
We are completely out of money."
"I can't believe how stupid you are Sel."
"Shut up Johnny
You don't understand a bit."
"Understand what Selsey Carnival?"
"Whatever it is, you don't understand it."
And that being said
He worries himself to the park
Yesterday seemed so bright
Today alas terminally dark.
To be short of cash is one thing
To owe money is worse still
And as Albert's always saying
To be in debt is to be ill.

"Wewl Johnny, you av got yourself into
wery big twouble, wery big oh yer! You
av fawlen fowl of a wery smart conman
but that aint an uncommon fing. Nowa
days undweds and farsands get taken for
a big wide, that cost em wery dear, oh yer.
All them insuwances that don't never pay

you wot they said, and don't never insuwer
no one but themselves, oh yer. Let me tewl
you, conmen are ever pwesent in awl
corners of ya life, that is untiwl you want ya
money. Then awl of a sudden ee aint wisible
and no one don't never see 'im again, and
thass a bweeding fack!!"

# 84

## Tears At Breakfast

For long days Selsey's inconsolable
And neurosis reigns supreme
She's lost without her plastic card
And her manners are obscene.

"Bay leaves, of course I don't want bay leaves
Don't call here anymore
We're not made a bloody money
Go to hell," then slams the door.

"Two thousand pounds for bay leaves
What do they think I am?"
"Selsey dear, they're bailiffs
Because you put us in a jam."

The bailiffs call next day
And then with a very big policeman
They take a multitude of valuables
And that dreadful flat screen television.

"Well Sel what did I keep saying?
Everything you want has to be paid for"
"Oh shut ya silly trap John
Don't be a depressing little bore."

Yesterday more bailiffs called
And more valuables were removed
And one thirty foot reception room
To say the least, looks pretty nude.

There's a few more tears at breakfast
And at last she does confide
She can't be seen out on the heath
And feels she wants to hide.

"Relieve me of these Blackheathens
They have wholegrain in their head
They have become an irksome drag
And a skin I'd like to shed.

"I can't abide these intellectuals
I take back every word I said
They think they're so damn clever
Spouting things that they have read.

"I think it's time you saw that bird
You so often talk about
I feel I am a prisoner in this house
And it's time that I got out.
I want a house and job up town
Where no one knows my name
With a more suitable occupation
That could possibly bring me fame."

Well that's quite a little number
But at least she wants an occupation
And with another income
It may smooth out aggravation.

Hero's in the top nursery
And the arboretum leaves are blowing
He whistles to the sky
And Sharheen's silhouette is showing.
There's no song of great enchantment

Or a promise of ransom
She's looking rather worn
And far from Sharheen the handsome.
But her manner is as sweets as ever
As she sits up in the trees
"Oh hello my dear friend
I'm here to give you what you please."

"Oh I beg of you be patient
I'm as foolish as a clown
I've let my wife get in the red
Now she wants a house and job up town."

"That my friend may be very hard
But I just think I may be able
To help you with your difficult task
And make your finances stable.

"Be careful my dear friend
I can only lead you to the door
My magic will not make you money
Even I've no gold in store."

"Thank you Sharheen, thank you again
I'll keep my fingers crossed
You give me hope again
When all I thought was lost."

Sharheen says nothing more
But climbs laboriously into the air
Then rapidly born away with leaves
Leaving Hero to think and stare.

# 85

## Last Hope

Hero arrives home and is surprised to find
A rather overweight MP
His arms around our Selsey's waist
And she's sitting on his knee.

They're looking very comfortable
With chocolate cake and tea
"Oh Johnny meet my new boss
This is Horace Percival Bee.

"He's the new minister for housing
And badly wants a PR girl."
The thought of working uptown
Puts my poor head in a whirl.

"He's been trying to trace Leo
And that's how he found me
He wants to buy our house
And has one uptown for me.

"His whole family's in finance
And are extremely well connected
I'll be paid a top rate salary
And the job is very well protected.

"For our house he will pay 1.5 million
And has a house in mind for 1.9
He will arrange a bridging loan
And things will work out fine.

"We'll be leaving in the morning
I'll ring you when it's through
We're dining with some banking friends
And have a lot of things to do."

Even steadfast Hero is joyful
With the thought of Selsey's pay
But quite speedily deflated
On hearing what Albert has to say.

"Selsey 'as got inwolved wiv a fwiendly
politician, she can't never 'av done such
a fing. Politicians don't never 'av fwiends
sept them ones they 'av a wery nasty abit
of stabbin in the back, oh yer. An even
though they look big an mighty, self-
important and stand on wery 'igh mowal
gwand, I liken em to cwocadiawls wot
they wesembawl in many ways. Their
lowness to the gwand and they're extwemely
fick skins, wery small bwain, and a wery big
mouff wot make em wery dangewous! An
wot is more despicable is their ability to
pwoduce cwocadile tears when it awl go
wrong, then put the blame onto everyone else
oh yer. And it's wery plain to see that they aint
never wed a page of 'istorwy in their 'ole life!
But what is more worse is the lefties that come
out of universities. Wot they learn in there put
em in confoosion their 'ole workin' life, oh yer!
But it don't stop em getting an inordinately big
piawl of money. Then take wery early wetirement
an then get a big farm in 'Arfordshire, wiv a lot of
pigs wot they are wery wewl sooted to bweeding,

224

and thass a fack!!"

But at last he gets the call
And from the cook indeed!
Phone number address and all
It took a bit of finding
But there she is in silk and sable
With a sleazy looking chauffeur
And a Rolls Royce in the stable.
A fine Queen Anne town house
Much sweetly gentrified
With a cook and cleaner living in
Downstairs in the gloomy hide.
Selsey stands beneath the fan light
"Oh Johnny dear, please don't come in
You can use the tradesman entrance
Down the steps there by the bin."
He walks through a small tunnel
And there he finds the bin
A wonderfully overgrown garden
That no one ever goes in.
It's walled long and slim
His heart is warmed to find such a treasure
With trees in sweet maturity
And potential out of measure.
Then a long way from the house
A door into a long forgotten dell
With a Victorian summer house
And an ancient rustic well.
A further door leads into a street
Somewhere far away
Slips the key into his pocket
He may need that some other day.
Soon back inside the house

The cook thinks he's the gardener
She feeds him on fine fare
And gives him scandal of the banker.
"A truthful man will always win
Providing he is given time
But pigs the world all over
Will always grunt like swine.
There be some pigs call at this house
Namely Horace Percival Bee
He's been disowned by his father
And puts government money where it shouldn't be."

When Selsey first arrived here
Her ambitions rose again
They smouldered for some time
Then of course burst into flame.
Upstairs it all looks smooth as silk
Bloated fat cats come and go
On a mountain of credit
And alcohol keeps up the flow.
Then of course the endless parties
That go on into the night
With Selsey and pop stars
Most look a dreadful sight.
Selsey's on the stage as usual
Swamped by dronish men
Pneumatic laughter and benign cliché
That are quite sickening to pen.
"Nice one... I like it!!
Who's a happy bunny then?"
It's the chauffeur this time
Treated far better than Hero
But still turns out to be a swine.

"First it was salacious glances
Then it was the most rude advances
Said he wanted much more pay
Of course, I sacked him right away.
He left the car in Oxford street
It was instantly towed away
I had to collect it from the pound
And my God I had to pay."

The whole charade it rumbles on
With its impending chaos
And the people selling bay leaves
Are discreetly paid off by Horace.
Selsey doesn't like Hero around
He's mostly in the attic bedroom
But now that winter's here
He likes the cosy downstairs gloom.
The cook he really likes
With her he's found a friend
And she's full of knowing wisdom
Says this job may be soon to end.
"There's whispers in the downstairs
About that Horace Percival Bee
That if it should leak upstairs
There shan't be no job for you and me!"
And sure enough one afternoon
They're downstairs having tea
When suddenly Horace comes in view
"For God's sake can you hide me."
Stuffed inside the cupboard with the brooms
Then the door is firmly locked
Hero quickly runs upstairs
A thousand paparazzi, he is pretty shocked.
No one wants the cad in house

A plan is quickly hatched
To the door down in the dell
Where he is rapidly despatched.
I think the press have sprung his game
Whatever that may be
So that's the very last appearance
Of the Right Honourable Percival Bee.
He very speedily resigned
And even quicker went off shore
Except for photos in the paper
You won't see him anymore.
But where will that leave Selsey?
It's not difficult to guess
No accountant need be called to say
Finance is in a pretty sorry mess.
Now that's a funny thing
He's left his holdall in the cupboard
Filled to the top with fifty pound notes
What a surprise for Mother Hubbard.
He gives a wad to the cook
Which she stuffs into her apron
Then hands the holdall in
To a policeman at the station.
Later he's dining with the cook and cleaner
In a strangely silent house
Then all at once they hear a sound
That surely is no mouse.
Selsey's frantically calling Johnny
Hero runs upstairs, it may be reconciliation
"Where's the bloody holdall?"
"I took it to the station."
"Cretinous imbecile, where did I ever find you?
You've lost me half a million."
Then comes a frenzied purple rage

And screams bounce off the ceiling
Then goes storming up the stairway
Throwing sundry valuables around
If her mother could but see her
Her performance would astound.

A somewhat calmer Selsey emerges
At breakfast in the morning
Although her crest has all but gone
She needs her pride and cash restoring.

"I've had the rich and famous
Come calling at my door
It's cost me money out of measure
So tell your bird I want some more.
I deserve a fancy title
And born a Libra of silver scales
I am surely good enough to be
A much loved princess for Wales.
I need a romantic castle
On a rock above the sky
Far away from silly people
And this noisy traffic rushing by.
So go and see that parrot of yours
Or I'll throw another rage
I want him at my beck and call
Right here inside a golden cage."

At the park there is some mirth
When they hear of Selsey's drama
Albert says, "You wait Johnny,
That gewls 'eading for 'er karma!
It sounds wery much like she 'as caught
that Amewican illness that 'as been

spweading wound the 'ol wewld. It's a mid
life cwisis twenty-first century western
woman's disease, oh yer. You always know
when they've got it, they aint never 'appy
wiv nuffin and can't never be cheered up,
and spend more money than they get, and
that aint never enough, but can be kept stable
wiv a Mascede Binze every year, and a lotta
'olidays in wery 'ot places, wiv stwong sunshine
oh yer! But a mate o mine oo live darn the Owd
Kent woad tewl me, that a stwong wight 'ander
can stop it in a minute. But as you know, I don't
'old wiv wiolence of any kind. In fack a wife
beater is the lowest form of life on the planet,
even lower than a politician, and thass a
bweeding fack!"

To call the bird Hero procrastinates
With this magic he should rejoice
There's awful shades of devil's dyke
But in the end he has no choice.
So to the top nursery again
"Oh why can't I tell Sharheen a lie?"
But with the deepest foreboding
Looks up and whistles to the sky.
For some time calls go unanswered
The sky grows dark, he can't think why
Now heavy snow is falling
Oh Kamikaze, Sharheen rockets from the sky.
Hero's quite benumbed with shock
And just stands there in swirling snow
"Sharheen may I tell you my request?
But alas I fear you already know.
My life is in a whirlpool of trouble

My wife's infected with a rage
And she's demanding so many things
And wants you in a golden cage."
Sharheen's eyes glow like molten silver
Sings a short demented song
Flies at speed in jagged circles
Something surely has gone wrong.
She's screaming like a peacock
And in and out the trees she's flying
Diving closely over Hero's head
The beating wings they're terrifying.
Strikes a branch in her blind fury
Comes cascading from up high
And with a thud lands by our Hero
With all glory gone and soon to die.
Hero rushes to pick her up
And gives her the kiss of life as he's been told
Looks into her lugubrious amber eyes
They soon turn grey and then grow cold.

"Cruel fate for fool I am
I've exchanged bad for even worse
Now your blood upon my hands
Oh but God would lift this curse."

**86**

## To Rise On Flowers

"Dear friend Sharheen the wonderful
Please I beg of you forgive me
I'll take you to the rhododendrons
And I'll make a grave for thee.
You asked for nothing but my prudence
You could have cursed or cried
Or showered me with golden tears
Instead without a word you died.
I'll dig your resting place with bare hands
Where fierce storms are turned to showers
Below the leaves in sweet scented mould
That you may rise again in flowers."

Coming home's a massive shock
The house was repossessed at 12 midday
It's completely boarded up
To get inside there's just no way.
The cook is sitting on the doorstep
Says that everything's gone, what an intrusion
"I'm sorry son, for you is destitution."
Hero still has the key to the dell
Finds his warm coat there in the shed
So whatever is in the summer house
That will have to be his bed
He lights a cheery little fire
Which helps keep away the frost
But it really is a dreadful night
At dawn he realises everything is lost

# 87

## Loss

Here in my lonely neglected dell
A flower like an angel grew by the rustic well
She rose proudly from the mossy floor
Such a thing I'd never seen before.
Her graceful line and colour she was rare
I could but sit awhile and stare
Next day I came to see my find
For she had entranced my mind.
Her bright face seemed not the same
She hung her head as if in sad shame
Yet I loved her in her new sorrow
I said to her I'll call tomorrow.
I did, but she had gone
Like the fairies or a half forgotten song
In spirit we shall always be together
For she lives here in my heart forever.

Here's our Hero, he is sleeping
In a summer house without a bed
Poor Hero his life repeats itself
He's in a house that's like a shed.
He's been waiting for his wife
But I think he waits in vain
And if he doesn't get a move on
He won't be seeing her again.
So on the fourth day he goes out searching
But then feels a melancholy pain
Relives the Sammy Selsey drama
And feels that desolation all again.

Then meets another in destitution
She once lived in cardboard city
And knows the ways of living rough
But for a vagrant girl she's pretty.
He takes her to a place of eating
And the two both have their fill
Tells her of his searching
And the reason why he's sad and ill.
And the magic bird Sharheen
And the state of things that be
First she smiles, then she laughs profusely
"Oh kids you've had too much LSD."
Later on she teaches him
To beg and scrounge, and duck and dive
And lots of other angles needed
When down and out, to stay alive.
She takes him to a church hostel
Where they both have a nice hot bath
And share their sad tales with others
Over tea and cakes they have a laugh.
She says never stay in a hostel
"If you do you're lost,"
So they both go to the summer house
Though the night is cruel with frost.
She's overjoyed to see the place
"God, what a gorgeous hide,"
They cook some sausages over the fire
Yes it's still good to be alive.
"I'll show you something I learned from a Russian
To keep you from dying on a frozen night
We lie down on this duvet, here in my pack
Both our coats on top and cuddle up tight."
And sure enough it's tolerably warm
So close he can feel her heart beat

Then she giggles a bit and wriggles a lot
But soon she's fast asleep.
Sleep won't come with this girl in his arms
There was no disguising she is pretty
But what is her story, and what does she want?
Her life such a waste, such a pity.

# 88

## Unhappy Night

Then the stars come tumbling down
And fall from the frosty sky
"Where are you going, why are you here," they said
"And why do you have that woman in bed?
Come out and tell us why?"

Then the stars dance about in the little dell
And they jeered as they passed the rustic well
"You don't know the woman you're sleeping with
You've lost your house and you can't find your spouse
Come careless boy tell us why?"

Then the pearly stars they called down Mars
And Mars glared down with an angry eye
"Why sleep with this woman you haven't wed
And why do you live in a garden shed
Come sinful boy, come tell us why?"

Then the storm clouds rush in from the west
And the stars climb back in the sky
He was glad when the stars had disappeared
And the heavens are snowing again
For how could he tell them why?

The night was not a happy one
But she was up at six, what heaven!
For when you sleep on the road
You get trampled on by seven.
The day is little better

The snow has turned to slush
So quickly find a warm café
Before the early morning rush.
They eat a hearty all day breakfast
The only meal that can be relied on
Then over another cup of tea they talk
Of Hero's future that must be dwelled on.
She says he really must find Selsey
So it's a strangely sad farewell
He gives her half his cash and a kiss
And of course the key to the dell.

## 89

### No Flowers In The Heart

"People passing don't really care
For they've never had to face despair
They don't know what shadows are cast
Upon the soul that lives in the past.
They haven't had a time without hope
Nights without bed, hot water and soap
You see, I live a life apart
Where no more flowers grow in the heart.
And with the ending of each day
My happy past slips further away
So kiss me now and say goodbye
That's my life, a kiss goodbye.
My love he was swept from me
I fled his death, what use a fallen tree
He left me memories, now grown dim
But I never wanted memories, I only wanted him."

An unseen hand guides Hero to the prefab
But what he sees is pretty shocking
Just the workmen and the digger
And a pile of rubble, once his everything.

**90**

## Hero's Folly

Selsey's sitting on the black and white
And she's not a very pretty sight
Yet he still loves her in her sorrows
And speaks to her of new tomorrows.
With one arm round his lost dove
Strokes the tendrils of her love
But she's in no mood for reconciliation
Indeed she's filled with aggravation.
"It's all your fault can't you see
You should have been more firm with me
Couldn't you see I was but a child?
God you make me so bloody wild.
I need a man that's strong in arm
To keep me safe and free from harm
Your wages wouldn't feed a shrimp
You're nothing but a working wimp.
It's all your fault, my fall from grace
If I could only smash your stupid face."
Hero's stung by such cruel cutting words
Feels a hateful boiling rage
A monster bursting from its cage
With one instant mighty blow
Sends her crashing down below.
Then sees hurt there in her face
And feels the pangs of his disgrace
Looks into her sad eyes
He feels the pain of her demise
Now full of shame and self surprise
Sits on the black and white and cries.

To the workmen on the digger
Hero's folly works like a trigger
Kicks him from the telly with a thud
Sends him sprawling in the mud.
Now Selsey's standing as if on the stage
She's in another purple rage
"You rotten low life cowardly brute
If I only had a gun I'd shoot."
From the skip a stick she snatches
Full of horrid barbs and catches
Hero feels he's soon to die
Her towering silhouette against the sky.
The workmen called out, "Go on girl
Give the little bastard hell."
Though it tears and cuts his hide
He feels nothing; the real pain is deep inside
One thought in his mind, this has to stop
He must get up and be on top.
With no small effort he's able to stand
And rest that spiteful stick from her hand
Once in his grasp, he's full of horror
The thing he holds was once his bower.
He staggers off towards the park
The snow clouds make the sky quite dark
And through his tears and blood and sorrow
Knows there can be no tomorrow.
And as Albert has so often said
"Sticks and stones can bweak your bones
But woman's words cut so deep
They don't never stop bweeding."

Snow is falling, wind is easterly
Stings his face, it's sharp and beastly
Motorists lean out and toot

As he staggers on his aimless route.
Children stare and cross the road
And hurry to their safe abode
A passing police car slows right down
"We ought to kick him out of town.
He looks such a disgraceful punk
No he's just another drunk, drive on."
Groups of teenage boys are coming
Think he's odd and queer and funny
One oaf laughs and kicks him in the tummy
But he walks on slightly reeling
His bankrupt heart is void of feeling
In love and hope he's lost conviction
This is reminiscent of a crucifixion.

At the park, things are no better. When Hero
relates his sad tale, Albert lets out a painful
wail. "You 'it 'er! Gawd almighty, ow come you
do such a fing? Because she make me angry
you tewl me, wewl you 'av made me wery
wery angry but I aint gonna 'it you am I. I've
'ad these wery bad pains in my chest all
bweeding day, now you tewl me you 'av 'it
poor littawl Selsey. You can't never 'av done
such a fing. Oh no! Listen 'ere Johnny, I am a
wery iwll man an' can die any time and there
is sumfing I 'av never tewl no one. Once I 'it a
man because ee was after the gewl that I was
sweet on. It all come abart wiv jealousy like.
Anyhow, ee fewll down and cwacked 'is scuwll
an even though I pwayed by 'is bed for fwee
days, ee died, and later I was put in pwison for
seven years. And she never mawied me what I
wanted, and ever since my 'art 'as been fiwlled

wiv wemorse and bitter 'atred awl my life, oh yer!
Now I've locked up, I fink you'd better go 'ome."
Then he turns and soon gone into the swirling snow.

"But I have no home, I have no wife
I have no house I have no life
Oh curse the endless cold and snow
There's no feelings left to hide
There can be nothing more, just suicide."
So now by the murky little lake
This awful decision he has to take.

He ponders for an endless while
Thinks he ought to dive, yes go in style.
As he ponders hears the voice of his mother
"Oh shameful boy, nought have you won
Your pledge to Sammy is now broken
For such a deed cannot be undone!"
Condemnation from his dead mother
Much worse by far by any other.
"Dear God, this Earth gives me no peace
Hell would be a pleasant release."

Now Hero's standing on the little bridge
Looking down on that ice dark space
Seems to think he sees his loved one
Thinks he sees her lovely face.

# 91

## <u>Loves Cinders</u>

"Oh sweetness if you only knew
I'd give my whole life back to you
And if I'd known all I should
I'd do it all again I would.
Give my soul for deprivation
My eyes for your temptation
Lend my ears for you to bend
All my cash for you to spend.
And give my pride for demolition
And my poor heart for mutilation
All for one burgeon year with you
Worth more than anything I knew.
Love's damp cinders no flame for me
We've broken forever, how silly can we be
And I have pondered to this last hour
How a love so sweet, has turned so sour."

Then into the darkness one almighty dive
But the ice it holds he's still alive
And carves a long and graceful slide
Only stopping at the other side.
He lies there winded and further cut
Cursing the padlock on the hut
And damnations to the ice that, snatched from him
A much craved release of death's oblivion.

# 92

## Hero's Soliloquy

"My broken promise to Sam, whom I am much
beholden
For his saintly silence is surely golden
In truth and on my own admission
I now stand lower than a politician.
Whose sore miscalculation, or despotic underhand
Can wreak financial pain throughout the land
Then brass it out, walk free and jolly
And possibly be knighted for their folly.
Yet my own levity caused by Christians taught
Equality and kind concern has disaster wrought
Now my father's gifts have all but been stolen
And percolated some unseen coffers already swollen.
I wouldn't be in this terminal demise
Had she given me some small degree of compromise
Why did she not hand me a fragment of appreciation
Or concede just one mutual evaluation.
These dread pitfalls could have been corrected
If my words and wishes had been respected
But no! She raged against my temperate heart
And without respect she cleaved our love apart.
Now I am here alone in guilt and half alive
For one careless fury, I am completely vilified
She came with love, guile and huge temptation
But hands me now a life of chronic dissipation."

# 93

## Love And Respect

Give me not of your love
For love comes with many barbs
Love has a wild sister, Lust
And another, tempestuous Passion.
Give me your respect ten fold
Then I will give you respect for respect
Love craves possession and kills freedom
Respect cannot possess so freedom's given.
Love is blinded by jealousy
Respect is all seeing and respects all
Love is envious of talent
Respect cannot envy and admires talent.
If love leaves, it is with spite
And when departed wants revenge
Respect cannot leave, it never invades
And has compassion even for the spiteful.
So give me your ten fold respect
And I will build walls around you
There within, a house with four towers
Two gardens, one of fruit and one of flowers.
And then with care and toil
We both shall enrich the soil
Then I will give you love in plenty
My love I'll give it all to you
With those incorrigible sisters two!

Now Hero finds he's locked in the park
As he trudges round in ever deepening snow
Unaware of the still beauty around him

He's slightly disconnected and feeling slow.
Oh for rest, oh for sleep
But at last, under the rhododendrons hanging low
He lies down in the dry leaves
At last there's shelter from the snow.
The mercury's reading 15 below
It's uncertain that he will see tomorrow
Here he's sleeping, dreaming, dying
Half from cold, but most from sorrow.
It is said that when you die
Your whole life goes rushing by
But our Hero's soon to find
Sweet memories come drifting through his mind.

**94**

## Poignant Dreams

In the cruel dark freezing night
Poignant cameos come glowing bright
A thousand mundane simple things
Like taking Sammy to the swings.
Sees Selsey waking from her trance
The day God gave her a second chance
Sees her by the bus stop smiling
Looking young and sweet beguiling.
She's holding Sammy like a posy
Under the sun drenched bower bright and rosy
Smells the perfume from the bower
In June's sweet honey hour.
Lives again that dark sad day
When poor Sammy slipped away
His first step, that first word
The most exciting sound he ever heard.

Ladies and Gentlemen please come out
Come help our Hero turn his fate about
There he is locked in the park
It's cold, snowing and pitch dark.
He's sick and sad, his heart is crying
For where he lies, he lays dying
If you see him treat him kindly
His only fault is loving blindly.

Come gentlemen will no one help our Hero
Well I thought as much of you
You're rotters all believe me

On good authority I know that to be true.

My own good mother told me so
So did the greengrocer's spouse
Also my big sister and her friend
And the barmaid at the public house.

Women say you're completely insensitive
Well of that there's little denying
You'd need to be to share a life
With all the insults and the crying.

And while we talk of insults
The girls have left you with the poo
Turned you into nappy changers
Get out boys, find another job to do!

Love of football makes you an awful trial
To your loved ones you're such bores
But listen to what Albert says
"Don't touch the pwam it aint no jobba yours."

When driving your car put your belt on
Sorry you can't give her a lift to the station
Pooh pooh that would be kerb crawling
Now you can't talk to half the nation.

These crowing prudes at Westminster
They think of you as crawling
I would call that sexist
You're not quite that appalling.

Gentlemen it is your job to fertilize these girls
So I'm afraid you gotta

But I've some happy news for you
Horny girls, they just love a rotter.

Why of course you can't help Hero
You still have the world upon your back
You still have the job of Atlas
But they've kicked away the jack.

So be warned kind gentlemen
They want your job and you to pay
Your feet removed you can't stand like men
And that's not all some would take away.

You the fair sex come help our Hero now
Ladies is there not a kind heart among you
Spoilt deceitful children all
On good authority I know that to be true.

The old man in the park, he told me so
The kids across the road, whose mother's done a
runner
Also Betty at the ballet school
And my friend and his big brother.

Whatever happened to sugar and spice?
If Hero were your sulky cat
Or that smelly dog of yours
Oh how you'd rally round for that.

You treat your dog like a lover
And your partner like a dog
Not a thought for those man-made goodies
Oh that you so covert and you hog.

**95**

## Modern Comforts

Think of your beloved motorcar
That takes you near and far
And the ubiquitous mobile phone
That comforts you when far from home.
And your complex central heating
In winter months, it takes some beating
Consider the time you save
With your toaster and your microwave.
Without your washing machine where would you be?
All that time it gives you free
Then there's that miraculous silver plane
That takes you off to sunny Spain.
A convenient caesarean especially for you
Plus the wonders of a boob job too.

All these things men have made for you
But do you love him just one bit?
No not a second thought
I suppose you must resent him for it.

You have your mind on that glass ceiling
And if you can't break through just sue
And lust for that top job
And give the poor tax payer another screw.

You tell us it's a great need
To bring back some bread and honey
But in truth we all know
It's your deep love of spending money.

If things aren't going as you like
You just cash the marriage in
Take that silver plane to Spain
And indulge yourself with sin.

Then if your plane should take a dive
"Oh my life's in such an awful mess,"
With just one minute to be alive
"Oh hell I've left the babies in the crèche."

## 96

### <u>Oil Rich Ladies</u>

Ladies we live in oil rich times
This gives you the feeling you run the world
One day fossil fuel will all be gone
Then we will need horsepower and manpower
And girl power will be back where it used to be.
There's not many horses not many men
If you read this and it makes you gasp
You may need a triple flint bypass
Come why can't you be as sweet as Selsey
Before she flew off her trolley
And indulged in timeless folly.
Your bosom be soft, why not your heart?
Sweet lips, why not your words be sweet?
Just be the mortal goddess that you are
You could still give the world a treat
I know you're busy but just one thing
Please don't act like a gannet
One or two babies, that's quite enough
Don't over-populate the planet.

Thank you ladies you look so good
Far better than you really should
With your passion for your work
Doing the jobs your love ones shirk
You're fine, it beats me where you get the time.

All those expensive hair dos
Endless perms and soapy shampoos
Your fingernails like polished wood

I've got to say they do look good.

All that shopping, all those queues
Just to find a pair of shoes
Were they such a perfect match?
Hell! This handbag has a faulty catch
Take it back, I think you should
Thanks all the same for looking good.

Well Hero nobody has time to help you
If you don't get up you're going to die
Ok you're upset by what your mother said
What are you, some sort of mummy's boy?
Elvis Presley he was mama's precious boy
Look what happened to him when the going got tough
Come on Johnny, you only hit her once
You lost it just once we've all done it once.
I know girls that would say she had it coming
Just look at you, lying down there
What did the vagrant girl tell you?
You're supposed to take the coat off and lay
underneath
Though she was broken, she's a smart kid
She ought to be saved, I liked her a lot
Listen if you don't get up Johnny Hero
You're going to spoil the whole show.
I promised my daughters a happy ending
The supporting actress has gone!
Now the Hero won't get up
This is supposed to be a poetic fantasy
Now you're turning it into a comedy
Alright then, don't get up!

## 97

### <u>I Have Loved Life</u>

"Let me die for I have loved life
So often I have risen before dawn
While others who may as well be dead
Miss the magic glow of a new Venus born
And lie unstirring in their bed.

"What is death, for it is only part of life
I have found, kissed and loved the rare flower
While others that are all but dead
Come with blind feet a clumsy shower
And on my precious sweetness tread.

"I have no loss by dying I have gained much in life
And from life's spring have drunk deep
While others with dull celibacy have court
For the half dead I can but weep
I've danced with the angels and done all I ought.

"If I die tell them that I have loved life
My joy I've pinned on the tallest star
My sorrows have seen the deep, but love life still
Life, how I wonder what you are
I've found no answer as no man ever will."

But where Hero lies in the snow
He lies close to the buried bird
He thinks there is a trumpet calling
That old familiar sound he's heard.

Maybe the cause of all his troubles
Was it Sharheen who spoiled the show?
The creditors or the borrowers
Maybe both, it's hard to know.

But there in his frozen torpor
Hears the song of great enchantment
"You're still young and handsome
I will pay you just one more ransom."

## 98

### A Sonnet To Sharheen

"Oh Sharheen you of generosity made whole
Humbled I before God and your sky
For without care of consequence I stole
And doled grievous havoc with your store
Grant me please my home as it was before.
Now in fearful reluctance of pardon I ask
My fair loves eyes smiling at the door
Then be joined in her warm passions green
Take her to my arms, and there not to be spurned
As one under the bower of our bond
With her red fury purged and all traces burned.
Her garlands restored, washed free of all ill conceit
May you cast a goodly spell on her desire
That she be in all seasons love's object to admire."

His feet are feeling oh so cold
His brain is struggling for the light
He's falling, thinks he's falling
Craves release from his endless plight.

Then again he's falling falling
Crash down on the floor
A policeman's climbing through the window
Hears Selsey's desperate calling at the door.

His mind still lingers with Sharheen
He's quite still and laying on his back
"Where is the bird? Where is..."
And can't believe he is back.
Sweet Sel she's soon with him

Cups his head in her firm hand
"Oh I'm sorry sweet box
I left the front door key on the stand."

Have you ever noticed in old movies?
Villains face down, Hero's face up when dying
Well our Hero isn't dying
He's glad to be alive and trying.

And very soon they're sitting by the fire
All sipping cups of tea
"It's all Albert's fault giving you penicillin
And you took it, how stupid can you be.

"You haven't woken for 48 hours
Just rolling about and moaning in that bed
And with such a temperature
I kept putting ice packs on your head."

Before the policeman leaves
He imparts his life's gem of wisdom
"Like myself Mr Smith, you're a lucky man
You have a bonny wife in your home.

"It's a blessing far beyond calculation
To have a good woman in your life
There's nothing I'd not do for mine
Everything I have I owe to my wife."

He stands by the open door, "Still snowing
I'm retiring in the spring, what luck
I'll spend more time in the garden
Nice strong rose over the door, I'd better duck."

"Happy Christmas!"

# 99

## Poor Sam

All is well in Drakefield Gardens
Hero's sitting up in bed
Eating crusty bread and kippers
In the house that's like a shed.

The room's all hung with decorations
Plus the charm of real logs burning
Selsey's manifestly full of joy
For in her heart bright hopes are stirring.

Outside it's hushed, and snow is falling
In the air there's Christmas calling
Traffic passing, skidding, sliding, breaking
Over insane humps of council making.

Commuters in their dismal pursuit of home
Hack through the homemade hell of Lewisham
Christmas trees adorn their ways
Bright coloured lights from windows blaze.

It's nine o'clock, the roads still snarled
June's hubby sits in his car feeling wild
June is worried, it's the office party, hubby's boss
Draws the curtain, and remembers what a wolf he was.

Now the frost is crisp, the snow has ceased
Polaris stares down from a starry feast
Shines down on a lonely grave
Of poor Sam that we could not save.

"Sel Sel I had a dream, it was a lovely spring day."
"Oh not now, I'll not run away
My poor head is full to bursting
With all the things I want to say.
I've bought you a lovely Christmas present
A coloured TV with flat screen
I've been saving up for ages
Then I saw them half price down Rye Lane
I just had to buy it, though I borrowed some cash from mum.
That old black and white, was becoming a bit troublesome
It's in Sammy's room, you wouldn't believe it
Looks like a little cinema now, go and have a look at it."

"June called today, I couldn't believe my eyes.
She's had a baby girl, she's such a lovely thing.
Big dark eyes and jet black hair just like her dad.
It made me feel quite broody. Oh yes she had
such a beautiful name, but it's slipped my mind.
She didn't even tell me she was pregnant. But
she's always been chubby, it just didn't show.
Now here's the really important thing; you
remember Albert was going in for a small op,
well he sent me a copy of his will. In my hand I
have a letter that shall make our lives much
better. Guess what. He's leaving me the cottage
on the hill. What heaven! Zing, a house with up
and down close by the railway into town. Isn't that
just wonderful Johnny! Oh yes, I've just remembered
the baby's name, it's Sharheen! It's Indian for falcon
or bird, something like that. Oh Johnny, what's wrong
why are you in tears. I know you're thinking of Sammy
aren't you.

"Oh look another Christmas card Johnny. It's
from Kingston Properties."
"Don't open it Sel, don't open it, it's just junk mail, put it
in the fire."
"Now get back into bed, you are in a funny mood, don't
know what came over you."
"Wanted 3-4 bedroom houses in this area."
"Well they won't be after this old shed. Oh look,
there's a lovely Christmas card with a picture of Jesus
and Mary in the stable with three lovely little baby
angels, and a little girl kneeling down with flowers and
a
smashing little poem, just listen."

**100**

## Christmas Day

Once a girl bought flowers, for a new born in a stable
And told of what she saw, as best as she was able
Around a simple bed of hay, three children stood
Each graced with a halo, like a glowing hood.
Feathered wings sprung from their back, I tell no lie
It was a mark of goodness, rather than to fly
There on the bed a mother and her baby boy
And in their eyes a glow of iridescent joy.
She said my name is Mary, then she smiled
But what name shall I give my darling little child
The first angel said Jesus, the second I think Christ
Mary smiled again, yes Jesus Christ, that does sound nice.
In turn they kissed the baby in the hay
Then the third angel said this is the very first Christmas Day.

"Move over Johnny, I want a little cuddle, you
don't know what that little Sharheen's done to me.
Oh Johnny you still look upset. It is Sammy isn't it?
Oh darling you're so sweet and emotional.
That's why I love you so much."